Editorial Project Manager
Erica N. Russikoff, M.A.

Editor in Chief
Karen J. Goldfluss, M.S. Ed.

Creative Director
Sarah M. Fournier

Illustrator
Mark Mason

Art Coordinator
Renée Mc Elwee

Cover Artist
Diem Pascarella

Imaging
Amanda R. Harter

Publisher
Mary D. Smith, M.S. Ed.

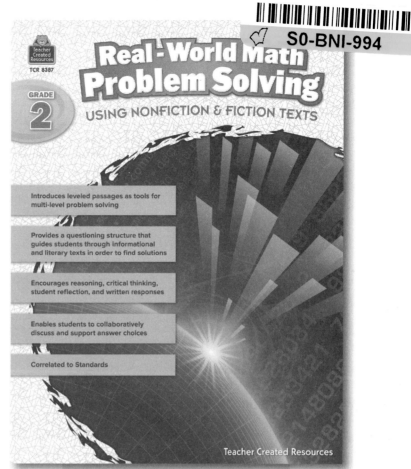

TCR 8387

Real-World Math Problem Solving

GRADE 2

USING NONFICTION & FICTION TEXTS

Introduces leveled passages as tools for multi-level problem solving

Provides a questioning structure that guides students through informational and literary texts in order to find solutions

Encourages reasoning, critical thinking, student reflection, and written responses

Enables students to collaboratively discuss and support answer choices

Correlated to Standards

Teacher Created Resources

Author

Tracie Heskett, M. Ed.

For correlations to the Common Core State Standards, see pages 107–112 of this book or visit *http://www.teachercreated.com/standards/*.

Teacher Created Resources

12621 Western Avenue
Garden Grove, CA 92841
www.teachercreated.com
ISBN: 978-1-4206-8387-5

©2016 Teacher Created Resources
Made in U.S.A.

Teacher Created Resources

Table of Contents

Introduction

Approaching Math Content— Today's Standards

The Common Core State Standards address several important goals in education:

- to prepare students for college and careers
- to develop critical-thinking and analytical skills students need for success
- to help teachers measure student progress and achievement throughout the year

The Common Core Mathematics Standards seek to provide teachers and students with focused mathematics instruction. The standards are designed to deepen students' understanding as they progress through grade levels and topics.

Mathematics is a subject in which concepts build in a progression. A strong foundation of basic concepts must be laid, beginning in the early grades. The Common Core State Standards recognize this learning sequence. Mathematical thinking is divided into several broad categories, referred to as "domains." Elementary grades address the same general domains, with specific standards for student understanding and achievement within each domain. For grades 1–5, these domains include Operations & Algebraic Thinking, Number & Operations in Base Ten, Number & Operations—Fractions (begins in grade 3), Measurement & Data, and Geometry.

It is important for students to understand the role mathematics plays in everyday life. The Common Core Mathematics Standards encourage students to apply their mathematical knowledge to real-world problems and situations. Teachers, in turn, assess student understanding and mastery of concepts by asking them to explain their thinking and justify their answers. Word problems provide students with opportunities for the practical application of mathematical concepts.

> This book presents word problems in a realistic setting. Students dig into the content of each "scenario" as they apply math concepts to solve multiple problems. Each unit is designed to encourage students to read for understanding, revisit content on a variety of levels, and use information as a tool for solving more complex problems.

Establishing Mathematical Practices

The Common Core Standards for Mathematical Practice (SMP) describe practices students can implement to help them engage with mathematical content. As your students work through the activities in this book, encourage them to develop these habits as they practice and develop problem-solving skills.

1. Make sense of problems and persevere in solving them.
2. Reason abstractly and quantitatively.
3. Construct viable arguments and critique the reasoning of others.
4. Model with mathematics.
5. Use appropriate tools strategically.
6. Attend to precision.
7. Look for and make use of structure.
8. Look for and express regularity in repeated reasoning.

These practices help students understand core mathematical concepts so they can apply a variety of strategies for successful problem solving. As students learn underlying principles, they will be able to . . .

- consider similar problems.
- represent problems in ways that make sense.
- justify conclusions and explain their reasoning.
- apply mathematics to practical situations.
- use technology to work with mathematics.
- explain concepts to other students.
- consider a broad overview of a problem.
- deviate from a known procedure to use an appropriate shortcut.
- reason and explain why a mathematical statement is true.
- explain and apply appropriate mathematical rules.

Help your students and their families find success. Work with administrators, other teachers, and parents to plan and hold math-coaching nights for parents. The tips on page 6 may be helpful for parents as they work with students at home. Consider photocopying the page to send home in students' homework folders to aid with math assignments. Additionally, prepare a visual aid to help parents understand students' work in math. Share this aid with parents at back-to-school night or on other occasions when they visit the classroom.

How to Use This Book

This book contains several mathematical problem-solving units. Each unit gives students the opportunity to practice and develop one or more essential mathematical skills. Units are grouped by domains—although within a unit, more than one domain may be addressed. Within each domain, math concepts build on one another, forming a foundation for student learning and understanding. In addition to the Common Core Mathematics Standards covered in this book, the passages that accompany each unit meet one or more English Language Arts Standards as they provide practice reading appropriate literature and nonfiction text.

About the Units

Each unit is three pages in length. Depending on the needs of your students, you may wish to introduce units in small-group or whole-class settings using a guided-to-independent approach. Reading the passages and responding to activities in collaborative groups allows students to share and support their problem-solving results. As an alternative, students can work independently and compare responses with others. Whichever method you choose, the reading and math activities will provide students with the tools they need to build mathematical knowledge for today's more rigorous math standards.

Page 1

All units begin with a reading passage that presents a mathematical problem or situation. Engaging nonfiction and fiction passages are included in the book. Passages are age-level appropriate and fall within a range of 420 to 650 on the Lexile scale.

Each passage incorporates information to be used for solving practical math problems. They also allow students to experience a variety of genres and make meaningful connections between math and reading.

Students practice reading skills as they read for understanding, revisit text on a variety of levels, and use passage information as a tool for solving more complex problems.

Sidebars provide tips to help students think about how to do the math. In addition, they offer tools or strategies students can use throughout the problem-solving process.

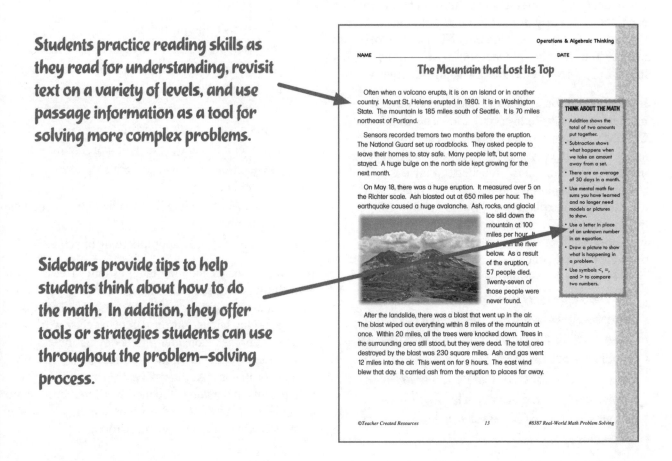

How to Use This Book (cont.)

About the Units (cont.)

Page 2

The second page of each unit introduces problem-solving tasks. Space is provided for students to draw pictures, work out their answers, write equations, show their work, and explain their thinking. Students are asked to use the unit passage to respond to reading content and investigate the text in order to find solutions to the problems on the page.

The questions require students to look back at the text for clues and information that relates to each question. They must then interpret this information in a way that helps them solve each task on the page. In doing so, students learn to support their responses with concrete evidence.

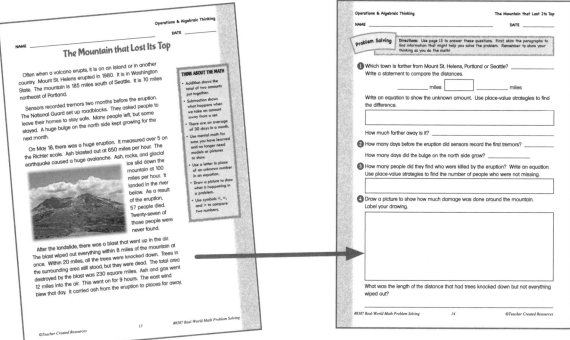

Page 3

The *Engage* option extends the mathematical situation with questions that allow students to look back at the reading passage and use critical-thinking skills.

The activities in this section strengthen students' comprehension skills by posing questions or situations for which further reflection of the text is required. Questions may be open-ended and require higher-level thinking skills and supported responses. Activities in this section focus on a combination of reading and math skills.

While students can respond independently to the activities on this page, you may wish to have them discuss their answers with a partner, in a small group, or with the entire class. This method can also provide closure to the unit.

The Path to Common Core Success: A Parent's Guide

Your child's success is measured by much more than numbers or grades. Being successful includes feeling confident and gaining practical skills to help students in life. The following tips will help you work with your child at home to understand the mathematics he or she is learning at school.

- Attend any curriculum or math-coaching nights offered by the school.
- Become familiar with the Standards for Mathematical Practice, which explain how students should apply math concepts and principles.
- Become familiar with the mathematical content standards, which explain what students should know about math and be able to do.
- Ask your child to explain the underlying concept of a math problem or the "main idea."
- Talk together about the core concept of a mathematical task to ensure your child understands it.
- Encourage your child to use concrete objects to model and demonstrate math problems.
- Talk with your child and help him or her to restate math problems in his or her own words.
- Have your child teach you one new strategy for solving a particular type of math problem.
- Discuss (parents and children) how a given strategy might be helpful to solve a particular problem.
- Discuss different ways a problem could be solved.
- Encourage your child to check that his or her solution is accurate and makes sense.
- Talk about ways math rules and concepts apply to specific problems.
- Explain how you used math that day at work or in your daily life.
- Help your child make connections between the day's homework and real-life applications.
- Support your child in the process of learning to think critically and analytically.
- Practice patience together with your child as you work on math together.
- Support your child as he or she develops additional reading skills.

NAME _____ DATE _____

The Blue Angels

What are the Blue Angels? They are a team of pilots and officers. They are from the Navy and Marines. There are 16 people on the team. Six pilots fly jets numbered 2 through 7. The Commanding Officer flies jet 1. He is called "the boss." Each pilot must have many hours of jet-flying time to be on the team. Pilots serve two years on the team. Some other officers serve three years.

The Blue Angels have been a team for more than 65 years. They started with 4 aircraft. Now they fly 6. They put on shows all over the country. Pilots fly the planes in patterns. They fly sideways and upside down. Members of the team talk with people from each community.

Pilots fly the planes in a diamond pattern. They may fly as close as 18 inches to another plane. Solo pilots fly up to 700 miles per hour during the show. The slowest speed they fly is 120 miles per hour. Many people come to watch these exciting air shows.

THINK ABOUT THE MATH

- Number words describe an amount of objects.

- An even number of objects can be put in pairs with nothing left over.

- Count by twos to determine if an amount is odd or even.

- Draw pictures to show what is happening in a problem.

- Use mental strategies to add or subtract numbers less than 20 by counting on, making a group of ten, or looking for easier or known sums such as doubles.

- Use symbols <, =, and > to compare two numbers.

NAME _____   DATE _____

Directions: Use page 7 to answer these questions. First, skim the paragraphs to find information that might help you solve the problem. Remember to show your thinking as you do the math!

1 Based on the information in the passage, how many jets might fly in the diamond pattern?

_____

Is there an even or an odd number of planes in the pattern we see in the sky?

_____

Draw a picture in the box to show this is true.

2 How many more planes fly now than when the team started?

_____

3 If there are 8 pilots on the team, how many members of the team help in other ways? Use mental math strategies to find the number of team members who do not fly.

_____

4 Is there an even or an odd number of pilots on the team? Draw a picture to show how you know.

5 Who serves longer on the team, pilots or other officers? Write a number statement to show your answer.

6 What is the difference between the fastest and slowest speeds during an air show? Group by hundreds and tens to find the difference in speed.

NAME _____   DATE _____

1 Who or what are the Blue Angels?

_____

_____

_____

2 What do they do?

_____

_____

_____

3 Why do you think they do this?

_____

_____

_____

4 In what pattern do the pilots fly the planes? Draw a picture to show how you think it might look.

```



```

5 What is the closest the pilots fly the planes to each other?

_____

Measure to find two things in the classroom that are the same distance apart as the planes. Write what you measured. _____

How would you describe this distance to someone? _____

_____

NAME _____   DATE _____

A Day at the Playground

THINK ABOUT THE MATH

- Addition shows the total of two groups of objects that are put together.
- Use subtraction to show what happens when we remove objects from a set.
- An even number of objects can be put in pairs with nothing left over.
- Count by twos to determine if a number of objects is even or odd.
- Use mental math for sums you have learned and no longer need models or pictures to show.
- Group by tens to add numbers up to 100.
- Use a letter in place of an unknown number in an equation.

Kaylee raced toward the playground, eager to try everything at once.

"Wait for me!" Ryan called, as he ran to two sets of bars that led to a platform. "I'll race you up the ladder."

"My ladder is taller, so you'll win." Kaylee stood and pointed at the bars.

"Count the number of bars. They're equal because they each have 13 steps. Ready, go!" Ryan started to climb.

Kaylee scooted up the steps and stood on the platform just as Ryan climbed over the top. She motioned to a set of monkey bars. "These have more horizontal bars than the ladders."

"Are you sure?" Ryan teased her, arms crossed on his chest.

"Count them for yourself." Kaylee swung out on the first bar. "This is a huge playground!" she called.

"Let's check out the slides next."

Kaylee jumped into the sawdust and wiped her hands on her jeans. "How many slides are there?"

Ryan turned around slowly in a circle. "One, two, three . . . six, I think."

"You can tell me all about them. I'm going to jump on the trampoline."

Kaylee bounced over to the edge of the trampoline when Ryan came up. "How many times did you jump?" he asked.

"Forty-seven times. Time for a drink of water." She trotted off to the water fountain on the side of the playground.

"Bet I can jump 20 times more than you!" Ryan stepped onto the trampoline.

She returned just as he finished jumping. "Let's sit on the swings and watch everyone else for a while."

NAME _____   DATE _____

Directions: Use page 10 to answer these questions. First, skim the paragraphs to find information that might help you solve the problem. Remember to show your thinking as you do the math!

1 What does an "equal" number of steps mean?

_____
_____

2 Does each ladder have an odd or an even number of steps? Explain how you know.

_____
_____

3 Draw a picture of a playground. It should include ladders, monkey bars, and slides.

```



```

• Color the vertical ladders blue.   • Color the horizontal monkey bars red.

4 How many slides are on your playground drawing? _____

Is there an odd or an even number of slides? _____

Are there more slides than ladders? How many more? _____

Write an equation with a symbol for the unknown number.

• Color the slides in your drawing green.

5 How many times did Ryan jump on the trampoline? _____

NAME _____   DATE _____

Engage   **Directions:** Refer to your drawing of the playground to think about and practice math skills.

1 Add things to your drawing of the playground.

What did you add? _____

2 Write math problems based on the things you added to your playground drawing.

Think about addition and subtraction problems.

Think about ways you used odd and even numbers of things in your drawing.

3 Share your math problems with classmates.

4 Copy a math problem that a classmate wrote.

Explain which math skills you used to solve this problem.

5 If possible, look at a real playground.

What objects in the playground can you count?

_____

_____

How do they compare with your drawing of the playground?

_____

_____

Write number sentences or use words to explain your thinking.

NAME _____   DATE _____

The Mountain that Lost Its Top

Often when a volcano erupts, it is on an island or in another country. Mount St. Helens erupted in 1980. It is in Washington State. The mountain is 185 miles south of Seattle. It is 70 miles northeast of Portland.

Sensors recorded tremors two months before the eruption. The National Guard set up roadblocks. They asked people to leave their homes to stay safe. Many people left, but some stayed. A huge bulge on the north side kept growing for the next month.

On May 18, there was a huge eruption. It measured over 5 on the Richter scale. Ash blasted out at 650 miles per hour. The earthquake caused a huge avalanche. Ash, rocks, and glacial

ice slid down the mountain at 100 miles per hour. It landed in the river below. As a result of the eruption, 57 people died. Twenty-seven of those people were never found.

After the landslide, there was a blast that went up in the air. The blast wiped out everything within 8 miles of the mountain at once. Within 20 miles, all the trees were knocked down. Trees in the surrounding area still stood, but they were dead. The total area destroyed by the blast was 230 square miles. Ash and gas went 12 miles into the air. This went on for 9 hours. The east wind blew that day. It carried ash from the eruption to places far away.

NAME _____   DATE _____

Directions: Use page 13 to answer these questions. First, skim the paragraphs to find information that might help you solve the problem. Remember to show your thinking as you do the math!

1 Which town is farther from Mount St. Helens, Portland or Seattle? _____
Write a statement to compare the distances.

_____ miles ☐ _____ miles

Write an equation to show the unknown amount. Use place-value strategies to find the difference.

How much farther away is it? _____

2 How many days before the eruption did sensors record the first tremors? _____

How many days did the bulge on the north side grow? _____

3 How many people did they find who were killed by the eruption? Write an equation. Use place-value strategies to find the number of people who were not missing.

4 Draw a picture to show how much damage was done around the mountain. Label your drawing.

What was the length of the distance that had trees knocked down but not everything wiped out?

NAME _____   DATE _____

Engage | **Directions:** Look back at the passage to review information about what happened during this eruption. Then, answer the questions below.

---

1 Why did the National Guard ask people to leave their homes? _____

_____

_____

2 How do we know the blast had a lot of force? _____

_____

_____

3 In this passage, what is an avalanche? _____

_____

_____

What happened to the ash, rock, and ice from the mountain? _____

_____

_____

4 Why did ash travel so far away from the mountain? _____

_____

_____

5 Mount St. Helens went from 9,600 feet high to 8,300 feet high in a few seconds. How much height did the mountain lose? Think about hundreds, tens, and ones to find the amount of height the mountain lost.

```



```

NAME _____   DATE _____

Spaceship Wars

"Will you play a game with me?" Makayla stood by the table where her brother sat drawing.

"Hm?" Anthony looked up. "Sure. We can test my new game." He finished coloring a spaceship. "Each card has a spaceship with a number. The number tells how much power the spaceship has."

Makayla sat down and looked through the cards. "Okay . . . this doesn't look very exciting."

"The spaceships go to war. You show one spaceship from your fleet . . ."

"What's a fleet?"

Anthony straightened the cards into a pile. He divided it into two equal piles and handed one to his sister. "This is your fleet. We each turn one spaceship card over. The spaceship with the most power wins."

"That means the greatest number?" Makayla turned over a card. "The winner takes both cards? I've played this game before."

"Not with these cool cards!" Anthony won and then picked up the two cards on the table to start a small pile next to him. The next two turns he also won the cards.

On the next turn, Makayla turned over a card with a power level of four. Anthony's spaceship had a level of four, too. "I don't remember what we do now," she said.

"We'll each deal five cards face down. That represents the forces sent into battle. Then we'll each turn over a sixth spaceship and see who wins." Makayla's last spaceship card had a level eight. The card Anthony turned over had a level five. Makayla scooped up all the cards from the battle with a grin.

NAME _____ DATE _____

Directions: Use page 16 to answer these questions. First, skim the paragraphs to find information that might help you solve the problem. Remember to show your thinking as you do the math!

1 At the end of the first three turns, how many cards had Anthony won "in battle"? _____

How many cards does the winner get in each round (including his or her own card)?

_____

Draw a visual model or write an equation to find the number of cards in his small pile.

2 Does Anthony have an odd or an even number of cards? How do you know?

_____

_____

3 What happened during the fourth turn? _____

Who won the cards on the fourth turn? _____

How many cards did that person win? _____

Draw a visual model or write an equation to find the total number of cards for that turn.

4 At the end of the game, Anthony had 27 cards. He made 36 spaceship cards in all. How many cards did Makayla have? Write an equation and group by tens to find out how many cards Makayla had.

Use numbers and a less than or greater than symbol to compare the number of cards each player had.

NAME _____ DATE _____

Directions: Create equations using the information given below about the cards and players in the game.

1 One player has an odd number of cards in his pile. The other player has an odd number of cards in her pile. Will the total number be odd or even? Draw pictures or write several equations to prove your answer.

2 One player has an odd number of cards in her pile. The other player has an even number of cards in his pile. Will the total number be odd or even? Draw pictures or write several equations to prove your answer.

3 If both players have an even number of cards in their piles and they add them together, will the total be an even number of cards or an odd number? Explain how you know.

_____

_____

_____

4 Write equations to show the total number of cards each person might have at the end of a game with Anthony's cards. Remember that Anthony made 36 cards.

5 Write equations to show the total number of cards each person might have at the end of a game with 52 cards in the deck.

NAME _____   DATE _____

Twelve Men of Gotham

Once upon a time, twelve men of Gotham went fishing. Some went into the water, and some stood on dry ground. On their way home, one of them said, "We took a risk wading in the water. I hope no one in our group drowned."

His comrade said, "Let us see about that. Twelve of us went fishing."

Each man counted the others. Everyone counted eleven, but none of the men counted himself.

"Alas!" they said to each other. "One of us has drowned." They went back to the brook where they were fishing. Then they looked up and down the brook for the one who was drowned, crying out.

A servant from the king's court came riding by. He asked what they were seeking and why they were so sad.

"Today we came fishing in this brook. There were twelve of us, and one has drowned."

"Count for me to see how many are left," said the servant.

One of the men counted eleven and did not count himself.

"What will you give me if I find the twelfth man?" asked the king's servant.

"Sir," they said, "we'll give you all the money we have."

"Give me the money." The servant began with the first man. He gave the fisherman a whack over the shoulders and said, "There is one." He thumped each man on the shoulder with the money bag as he counted them. When he came to the last man, the servant gave him a good smack and said, "Here is the twelfth man."

"Oh, thank you," they all said. "You have found our companion."

> ## THINK ABOUT THE MATH
>
> - An even number of objects can be counted by twos.
> - An even number of objects can be put in pairs with nothing left over.
> - Two equal numbers added together will have an even number as their sum.
> - An array is an arrangement of objects in equal-sized rows.
> - Use a number line to count by twos or fives.
> - Use an array to count groups of objects with an equal amount in each group.
> - Use known math facts to solve math problems.

NAME _____   DATE _____

Problem Solving   **Directions:** Use page 19 to answer these questions. First, skim the paragraphs to find information that might help you solve the problem. Remember to show your thinking as you do the math!

1 How many men went fishing? _____

2 Did an odd or an even number of men go fishing? How do you know?

_____

_____

Draw a picture or use a number line to show your thinking.

```
┌────────────────────────────────────────────────────────────┐
│                                                              │
│                                                              │
│                                                              │
│                                                              │
│                                                              │
│                                                              │
└────────────────────────────────────────────────────────────┘
```

3 How many men did they think were left at the end of the day? _____

Which mental math strategy did you use to answer the question? Why did you choose this strategy?

_____

_____

_____

4 Why did they think that one person had drowned? Draw a picture, use a number line, or write a true number statement to explain your answer.

```
┌────────────────────────────────────────────────────────────┐
│                                                              │
│                                                              │
│                                                              │
│                                                              │
│                                                              │
└────────────────────────────────────────────────────────────┘
```

5 How did the king's servant find the twelfth man? _____

_____

_____

NAME _____   DATE _____

Engage | **Directions:** Use the information in the reading passage and questions below to find the answers to the math problems.

1 If each man had five dollars, how much money did the king's servant receive in all? Count by fives, use a number line, or draw an array to find the answer.

2 How many men would contribute five dollars each if 3 men left their money bags at home? Use mental math or write an equation.

How much money would the king's servant receive? Count by fives or draw an array to find the answer.

3 Half of the fishermen caught 3 fish each. Half of the fishermen equals how many? _____

Draw an array and count by threes to find the total number of fish caught.

How many fish did they catch in all? _____

4 If each man brought a friend, how many people would be in the fishing group? Count by twos or draw an array to show your work.

With the king's servant and the friends, how many men would be in the large group in all? _____

Is this an odd or an even number of people? How do you know?

_____

_____

NAME _____   DATE _____

A Balloon Ride

Imagine a balloon large enough to lift a person into the air. It flies because hot air rises and cold air sinks. Hot-air balloons float in the air. A hot-air balloon has 3 parts. People ride in the *basket*. It has sides about 3 feet high. This allows people to see out yet still be safe. Only one person might fit in a small basket. Large balloons can carry up to 15 people.

A *burner* heats air that goes into the balloon. Hot air rises; when the balloon is full of hot air, it goes up in the air. The colorful fabric is called the *envelope*. It holds the hot air. The pilot cannot steer the balloon. He or she guides it by heating or cooling the air in the balloon to go up or down. Different layers of air might move in different directions. This is how he or she gets the balloon to go where he or she wants it to go. Pilots also study the wind before they even start.

A balloon ride lasts about 60 minutes. The distance it travels depends on wind speed. The balloon might go a couple of miles or as many as 10. Often a balloon floats up about 500 feet in the air. It can go up to 2,000 feet. A balloon can last for 500 flying hours.

NAME _____   DATE _____

Problem Solving   **Directions:** Use page 22 to answer these questions. First, skim the paragraphs to find information that might help you solve the problem. Remember to show your thinking as you do the math!

1 A group of people want to take a balloon ride. There is an even number of people in the group. What is the most people that would fit in one large balloon? Draw a visual model to find the number of people.

```



```

2 What is the difference between the greatest and the least number of people who can go on a balloon ride? Use mental math to find the answer.

_____

_____

3 Sometimes there are hot-air balloon festivals. One balloon might have 12 people and another might have 7 people. How many people would there be in those two balloons? Use mental math to find the answer.

_____

4 How tall are the sides of the basket? _____

How tall is that in inches? _____

How tall are you? _____

How much taller are you than the sides of the basket? _____

Use a number line or write an equation to find the answer.

5 How long is one balloon ride in hours? _____

How far does it go in that amount of time? _____

6 How many 1-hour flights can one balloon make? _____

NAME _____   DATE _____

1 What are the three parts of a hot-air balloon? _____

_____

2 Which part is the colorful fabric of the balloon? _____

Why does it have that name? _____

_____

_____

3 What makes the balloon go up in the air? _____

How does a pilot steer the balloon? _____

_____

_____

4 What affects the distance a balloon can travel? _____

_____

5 What kinds of things might you see on a hot-air balloon ride? Draw a picture to go with
your explanation.

_____

_____

_____

_____

_____

_____

_____

_____

NAME _____   DATE _____

Waving the Flag

Liam hopped up and down. "Will I be able to see the parade, Dad?"

"Yes. If you stand on the rock wall against the fence, I'll hold you."

A band marched by, playing music. Then Liam saw people riding horses. The horses held their heads high and pranced. Two of the horseback riders carried flags. "There's the United States flag," he pointed. "But what's that other flag? It has the same colors."

"That's the first flag our country had. It shows the number of original colonies." Liam's dad handed him a small cloth flag.

Liam waved the flag and watched the parade. "Here come more flags! They all look sort of like our flag, but not exactly."

His dad looked closely. "Those are flags we've had through the years. Each has a different number of stars to represent the number of states. As our country has grown, the flag has changed."

"How many different flags have there been?"

"Twenty-seven. How many did you see in the parade?"

Liam turned his head and tried to count those that had passed by. "I'm not sure, but there were a lot."

The breeze caught Liam's little flag. "Do you know how many stars and stripes our flag has?" His dad held the flag still so Liam could see it.

Liam thought for a moment. "Thirteen stripes for the original colonies. Fifty stars for each of the fifty states."

"Yes," his dad nodded. "We're proud of our flag and our country." He took Liam's flag and waved it high.

THINK ABOUT THE MATH

- An even number of objects can be counted by twos.
- We skip-count when we count by twos, fives, tens, or any other number.
- An array is an arrangement of rows of equal objects.
- Rows go from left to right.
- Use skip-counting to find the total number of objects in an array.
- Use mental math or add multiples of ten to find the total number of objects in an array.
- Use a letter in place of an unknown number in an equation.

NAME _____   DATE _____

Directions: Use page 25 to answer these questions. First, skim the paragraphs to find information that might help you solve the problem. Remember to show your thinking as you do the math!

1 Why are there 13 stripes on the flag? _____

_____

Are there an odd or an even number of stripes? _____

2 How many states have been added to the original colonies? Write an equation to find the number of added states.

┌──┐
│   │
│   │
│   │
│   │
│   │
└──┘

3 Are there an even or an odd number of states? _____

4 Look at the picture of the flag on the previous page.

How many rows of stars do you see? _____

How many rows have 5 stars? _____

How many rows have 6 stars? _____

Show how you can prove there are 50 stars in all.

┌──┐
│   │
│   │
│   │
│   │
│   │
│   │
└──┘

5 Which flag had an equal number of stars and stripes? _____

_____

6 Liam wasn't sure how many flags he saw. If the parade had one of each flag from the United States' history, how many flags would he count? _____

NAME _____ DATE _____

> **Engage** | **Directions:** Read books, look at Internet sites, and talk with classmates to learn more about the history of the United States flag. Then, answer the questions below.

1 Choose one flag from the United States' history to draw in the box. How many stars does it have? _____

How many states were in the Union at that time? _____

2 Why has the flag changed through the years? _____

_____

_____

_____

3 Which flag design do you like the best and find most interesting? Why? Describe the flag and draw a picture. Tell why it is important to you.

_____

_____

_____

_____

_____

4 Pretend you could design a new flag for the United States. How would you show the number of states? Draw your design and explain it to a classmate.

NAME _____   DATE _____

Benjamin Banneker: Math Whiz

People have watched the moon and stars move in the sky for hundreds of years. They know the moon affects high and low tides in the ocean. Some people study these things closely. They make charts and tables to help other people. Benjamin Banneker studied the stars. He was good at math, and he printed information to help farmers and other people.

Benjamin lived during the time of George Washington. He grew up on a 100-acre farm. When he was 21, he made a wall clock that would strike on the hour. He may have seen the works of a pocket watch, but he had never seen a clock. His clock worked for the rest of his life. Benjamin lived to be 74 years old.

He worked the farm until he was 59. Then his health forced him to retire. This gave him more time to study the stars. George Washington wanted people to survey the land for the nation's new capital. Benjamin got the job. He had to lie on his back at night to use the instruments and make notes. The job lasted 3 months. At the end, he was paid $60.

In 1792, Benjamin had an almanac published. It was a book with tide tables and charts of the moon and sun. It also had the times of sunrises and sunsets. He wrote almanacs and had them published for the next five years. Different people printed them. There were 28 editions made in all. Benjamin was 66 when his last almanac was printed, but he kept notes and made charts every year until he died.

NAME _____   DATE _____

Problem Solving

Directions: Use page 28 to answer these questions. First, skim the paragraphs to find information that might help you solve the problem. Remember to show your thinking as you do the math!

1 How big was the farm where Benjamin lived? _____ A common city block is about 2 acres. How many city blocks would fit on Benjamin's farm? _____

Which strategy did you use to find the number of city blocks? Why did you choose this strategy?

_____

_____

2 How many years after he made the wall clock did Benjamin stop working the farm? Write an equation.

_____

How many years did Benjamin live after he retired from the farm? Write an equation.

_____

What strategies did you use to find the unknown number in these questions?

_____

_____

3 How much did Benjamin make each month when he surveyed for George Washington? Draw an array showing 3 months to find out how much he made each month.

_____

4 What year was Benjamin's last almanac published? _____

5 How many more years after that did he take notes and make charts? Write an equation.

_____

NAME _____   DATE _____

Engage   **Directions:** Think about the things Benjamin Banneker did during his life. Refer to the passage as necessary to answer the questions below.

1 What is an almanac? _____

_____

_____

2 What job did Benjamin do for George Washington? _____

_____

_____

3 To "survey" means to measure an area to make a map or plan. How did Benjamin's work at night help George Washington make a new capital city?

_____

_____

_____

4 What does it mean to say Benjamin had almanacs **published** for five years?

_____

_____

_____

5 Why is it important to remember Benjamin Banneker? _____

_____

_____

_____

_____

NAME _____   DATE _____

Riding the School Bus

Perhaps you ride a bus to school. Some students ride buses to go on field trips. There are also activity buses that carry students to sports events.

School buses come in all sizes. The smallest buses carry 20 or 30 students. There are 5 rows of seats. A mid-size bus carries 48 students. It has 8 rows of seats. The next-largest size holds about 72 students. This is the most common size for a school bus. One model has 12 rows of seats. In between the rows of seats on each bus is an aisle. Kids walk down the aisle to find a seat.

Special-needs buses have spaces for wheelchairs. A lift carries wheelchairs up to the bus. There are not as many seats, and the bus is much smaller. These buses often have seat belts.

Each size bus has a different length. Short buses are about 26 feet long. A mid-size bus might be 28 feet long. Large buses range from 35 to 38 feet in length.

THINK ABOUT THE MATH

- An array is an arrangement of items in equal-sized rows.

- An aisle is a walkway between seats as in a bus, train, or airplane.

- Half of the seats are on one side of the aisle and half are on the other side.

- Divide a number in half by separating the total amount into two equal groups.

- Use visual models to divide a group of objects into two equal halves.

- Draw an array to find how many objects are in each equal-sized group.

- Use place-value strategies to compare lengths of objects that are more than 10 measurement units in length.

NAME _____   DATE _____

Directions: Use page 31 to answer these questions. First, skim the paragraphs to find information that might help you solve the problem. Remember to show your thinking as you do the math!

1 Draw an outline of a small school bus showing the seats inside.

How many rows are in your picture? _____

How many people can sit in each row? _____

What is another word for your picture of rows? _____

2 Draw an array to show how many kids can sit in a mid-size bus.

How many rows are in your array? _____ How many kids can sit in each row? _____

3 The most common size school bus holds _____ students.

Draw an array to show this bus. Include an aisle (space) in the middle of each row.

How many rows of seats are on this bus? _____

How many kids can sit in each row? _____

How many seats are there on each side of the aisle? _____

4 What is the difference in length between the longest and shortest size of school bus? _____

What is the difference between the largest school bus and the mid-size bus? _____

5 Write the lengths of the types of school buses in order from shortest to longest.

➜

➜

NAME _____   DATE _____

| Engage | **Directions:** Think about what you read and what you already know about school buses. Then, answer the questions below. |

1 What are some reasons children ride a school bus? _____

_____

_____

_____

2 What are some things you would find on a school bus? _____

_____

_____

_____

3 What features are on a special-needs bus? _____

_____

_____

_____

4 How far away from school do you think children can live before they have to take a bus?

_____

_____

_____

5 Do you think all school buses should have seat belts? Why or why not? _____

_____

_____

_____

_____

NAME _____   DATE _____

The Pied Piper*

THINK ABOUT THE MATH

- One thousand is equal to ten groups of one hundred.
- Read number words to identify numbers in a problem.
- To add or subtract three-digit numbers, add or subtract hundreds and hundreds, tens and tens, ones and ones.
- Put together or take apart numbers to make tens or hundreds to add or subtract three-digit numbers.
- Use numerals to write large numbers to 1,000.
- Use place-value strategies to find differences between two dates.

Alas, alas for Hamelin!
The Mayor sent to the East and West.
He sent to the North and South.
To make an offer to the Piper,
by word of mouth.
He would give him silver and gold.
If he'd come back the same way he had left town.
And bring the children back around.
They soon saw it was a lost endeavor.
The Piper and dancers were gone forever.
They made a decree for all town records.
That they should show the date and year.
And also have these words appear.
The number of years since what happened here.
The twenty-second of July,
thirteen hundred and seventy-six.
To help people remember the children's retreat,
they called the lane Pied Piper's Street.
No one could play the pipe or horn,
or sure his labor would meet with scorn.
The eating places could not meet,
gladness on this solemn street.
They wrote the story on a column.
And wrote on the church window to show
the story, so all would know.
Their children were stolen away,
and the writing stands to this very day.

*Adapted from "Pied Piper of Hamelin," stanza 14, by Robert Browning, 1888

NAME _____   DATE _____

Problem Solving   **Directions:** Use page 34 to answer these questions. First, skim the poem to find information that might help you solve the problem. Remember to show your thinking as you do the math!

1 What is today's date? _____ _____, _____

2 Which number words tell you the date this happened?

The _____ of July

thirteen hundred and _____

Write the date.

_____ _____, _____

3 How many years ago did this happen? Write an equation.

4 Robert Browning wrote this poem in 1888. How many years ago did he write the poem? Write an equation.

NAME _____ DATE _____

Directions: Read the poem again and think about ways math is used in the poem. Then, answer the questions below.

1 In which directions did the Mayor search for the Piper?

_____

Based on what you know about maps, what does your answer tell you?

_____

2 What time of year did this happen? How do you know?

_____

3 What did the Mayor offer the Pied Piper for the return of the children?

_____

4 Earlier in the poem it says the Pied Piper asked for a thousand guilders for the return of the children. A thousand guilders is a lot of money. With half of that amount, the council could buy food to fill the cellar.

How much money would it take to restock the cellar? Group by hundreds to find half of one thousand.

```



```

5 At one point earlier in the poem the people offered the Pied Piper 50 guilders for the children. What is the difference between this amount and the amount the Pied Piper wanted?

Amount the Pied Piper wanted: _____   Amount the people offered: _____

Draw a picture or write an equation to find the difference in amounts.

```



```

NAME _____   DATE _____

Robin Hood and the Sad Knight

One day after the midday meal, Robin and his men hid near the road. A knight passed by with so much sorrow it seemed even his horse grieved.

Robin Hood approached him. "Hold, Sir Knight."

"Who are you, to stop a traveler? And what do you want of me?" asked the Knight.

Robin gave his name. "If you will go with me to Sherwood Forest, I will give you a great feast."

"You are very kind," said the Knight. "But let me pass in peace, I would not be a pleasant guest."

"Guests do not often come to us deep in the forest. My friends and I seek companionship. But I must tell you we count on our guests paying."

"I have no money."

Robin held the man's horse and whistled. Fourscore men ran to where Robin stood with the Knight. "These are my merry men. Tell me what money you do have."

The Knight said nothing, but his cheeks grew red. "I tell you the truth, I have ten shillings and that is all. Here, see for yourself." He held out his money bag to Robin.

"Put your bag away," said Robin. "I seek to aid those in sorrow. Come."

"You are truly kind," said the Knight, "but I do not think you can cure my troubles." He led his horse and followed Robin.

"Can you tell me?" Robin said as they walked along together.

"I owe a debt. If I do not pay the money in three days, I will lose my castle and land." The Knight told Robin the story. His twenty-year-old son had won at the jousts the year before. Sadly, he had an accident in which Sir Walter had died. Sir Walter's friends put the Knight's son in prison. The Knight paid six hundred pounds in gold to free his son. "They have since come after me for more money, and I had to pawn my lands."

"How much do you still owe?"

"Four hundred pounds," said the Knight.

Robin smacked his fist against his thigh. "What will happen if you lose your lands?"

"It is for my wife's sake I wish to save my estate. If I lose my land she will have to live with her family in charity. If that happens I would cross the ocean to fight with my son in the battles there."

They came to the glen where the rest of Robin's band waited. "Cheer up, Sir Knight," said Robin. "I may be able to help you."

> ## THINK ABOUT THE MATH
> - Think of a shilling as 12 pennies.
> - Think of a pound as 20 shillings.
> - A score is twenty units or objects.
> - Group by tens to work with numbers up to 100.
> - Group by hundreds to work with numbers greater than 100.
> - Draw an array to understand groups of equal amounts.

NAME _____   DATE _____

Problem Solving

Directions: Use page 37 to answer these questions. First, skim the paragraphs to find information that might help you solve the problem. Remember to show your thinking as you do the math!

1 How many men joined Robin Hood on the road? Group by tens or twenties, use a number line, or draw an array to find the answer.

2 How much money does the Knight have now? _____

How many pennies is that? Draw a picture and group by tens or use a number line to find the number of pennies.

3 How many pounds did the Knight pay to free his son from prison? _____

4 How many more pounds did the Knight owe to reclaim his lands? _____

5 How much money would the Knight pay his enemies in all? Count by 100s or write an equation to find the total amount of money the Knight had to pay.

NAME _____   DATE _____

1 How much did Robin Hood charge the Knight to come to the feast? _____

_____

_____

_____

2 Where did the Knight's son go after he was freed from prison? _____

_____

_____

_____

3 What will happen if the Knight loses his lands? _____

_____

_____

_____

4 Why do you think Robin Hood likes to help those who are in trouble? _____

_____

_____

_____

_____

5 How do you think Robin Hood might help the Knight? _____

_____

_____

_____

_____

NAME _____   DATE _____

The First Post Office

George Washington was our first president. In 1792, he signed a law. It was called the Postal Service Act. Before this law, people carried letters from place to place. The law made it so mail routes could be set up. Things other than letters could be mailed. It became against the law to open mail for someone else.

The cost to mail a letter depended on how far the letter would travel. The lowest rate was six cents for a letter. Mail that went 30 miles or less had this rate. Letters that traveled 450 miles or more cost 25 cents. These rates were for letters that weighed one half ounce or less. Almost 100 years later, rates changed. Now the rates are for a letter that weighs one ounce or less. In 2015, it cost 49 cents to mail a letter anywhere in the U.S.

NAME _____   DATE _____

Directions: Use page 40 to answer these questions. First, skim the paragraphs to find information that might help you solve the problem. Remember to show your thinking as you do the math!

1 What is the **difference** in the cost to mail a letter in 2015 and the cost when the U.S. Postal Service was first set up?

Cost to mail a letter in 2015: _____

Lowest cost when the U.S. Postal Service was first set up: _____

Write an equation to find the difference in cost.

```



```

Write an equation to check your work with addition. _____ + _____ = _____

2 What is the **difference** in the cost to mail a letter that would go a greater distance and the cost to mail a letter that would go a shorter distance?

Cost for a letter that would go a *greater* distance: _____

Cost for a letter that would go a *shorter* distance: _____

Write an equation to find the difference in cost.

```



```

Write an equation to check your work with addition. _____ + _____ = _____

3 What was the **difference** in distances that were used to figure the cost of a letter?

Shortest distance for 25¢: _____ miles   *Greatest* distance for 6¢: _____ miles

Write an equation to find the difference in distance.

```



```

4 How many years has it been since Washington signed the Postal Service Act? How can you solve this problem?

_____

_____

NAME _____   DATE _____

> **Engage** | **Directions:** Discuss with classmates the differences between the post office service long ago and our mail service today. Then, answer the questions below.

1 Why do you think it cost more for a letter to go farther in 1792? _____

_____

_____

_____

2 Why is the cost to mail a letter now the same no matter how far it goes? _____

_____

_____

_____

3 Why is it important to think about these differences in the cost of a letter? _____

_____

_____

_____

4 Why do you think the cost to mail a letter has increased? _____

_____

_____

_____

_____

5 What does it mean to say the cost has increased? _____

_____

_____

_____

NAME _____ DATE _____

Sleeping Lemurs

Many animals hibernate in the winter. Their bodies change during this time. Their heart rates slow down. They do not breathe as often. Their bodies cool down.

Fat-tailed dwarf lemurs live on an island off the coast of Africa. They hibernate for several months. In June and July, the temperature can drop as low as 41 degrees. It usually stays around 60 degrees during this cold time of the year.

The lemurs find holes in trees. They settle in to wait until the rains return. Then food will be available again.

Fat-tailed dwarf lemurs do not eat while they hibernate. They live off the fat stored in their tails. This is where their name comes from. During this time, they lose almost half of their body weight. They weigh over 200 grams when they start to hibernate. When the rains start in November, they weigh less than 150 grams.

Lemurs take one breath every 20 minutes when they hibernate. Their heart beats 6 times a minute. When they are awake, their heart beats 120 times a minute.

Scientists would like to learn more about how lemurs sleep when they hibernate. Animals need deep sleep to stay alive. It looks as though lemurs do not get this kind of sleep when they hibernate. They only sleep in the dream sleep stage.

The way lemurs hibernate is interesting to study. Scientists wonder if humans could hibernate in the future. This would be useful for long surgeries and extended space travel.

THINK ABOUT THE MATH

- Use subtraction and place-value strategies to find differences between numbers.
- Finding differences helps us compare information to learn about things.
- Look at the number of hundreds, tens, and ones to add or subtract two- and three-digit numbers.
- Subtract tens and tens, and ones and ones to find the difference between two two-digit numbers.
- Use addition to check subtraction.
- Write equations to show how to find the difference between two numbers.
- Use mental math or a hundreds chart to add or subtract multiples of ten.
- Use expanded form to add or subtract three-digit numbers.

NAME _____   DATE _____

Problem Solving **Directions:** Use page 43 to answer these questions. First, skim the paragraphs to find information that might help you solve the problem. Remember to show your thinking as you do the math!

1 Temperatures in Africa are different than they are in the United States.

How low can the temperature drop in Africa? _____

What is the normal winter temperature in Africa? _____

How much colder than normal is the low temperature in Africa? _____

2 March is the warmest month. It can be as warm as 90 degrees. What is the difference between the high and low temperatures? Write an equation to find the difference.

3 What is the difference between a lemur's normal heartbeat and its heartbeat when it hibernates?

_____

_____

4 One lemur weighed 217 grams in March. It weighed 142 grams in November when it came out of hibernation. How much weight did it lose? Use expanded notation to find the difference.

NAME _____   DATE _____

Engage | **Directions:** Discuss with classmates what you learned about how lemurs hibernate. Then, answer the questions below.

1 What are some ways the lemur's body changes when it hibernates? _____

_____

_____

_____

_____

2 Why is this kind of lemur called a fat-tailed dwarf lemur? _____

_____

_____

_____

3 Why does the lemur hibernate? _____

_____

_____

_____

4 What is something interesting about the way this animal hibernates? _____

_____

_____

_____

5 Why do scientists want to study how lemurs hibernate? _____

_____

_____

_____

NAME _____   DATE _____

Lou Gehrig: The Iron Horse of Baseball

Lou Gehrig played baseball in the shadow of Babe Ruth. Lou Gehrig wore uniform number 4 for the New York Yankees. Babe Ruth wore uniform number 3. Babe Ruth was outgoing. Gehrig was quiet and humble. But Gehrig is also in the Hall of Fame. He played 14 full seasons in a row without missing a game. This works out to be over 2,000 games.

During his career, Gehrig hit 493 home runs. In 1927, he hit 47 home runs. That same year he scored 149 runs. Eight times he had at least 200 hits in a season. One year, Lou batted in 185 runs. That same year, Babe Ruth batted in 162 runs. Several times Lou led the league in runs and hits. He played on seven All-Star teams. Later, he was voted greatest first baseman of all time.

His long-playing streak came to an end in 1939. Lou took himself out of the lineup. He had a bad start to the season. He had a mysterious illness. It made his nerves and muscles weak. He had ALS. It became known as Lou Gehrig's disease.

More than one person has summed up Lou Gehrig's career. One of his teammates said, "He just went out and did his job every day."

NAME _____   DATE _____

Problem Solving

Directions: Use page 46 to answer these questions. First, skim the paragraphs to find information that might help you solve the problem. Remember to show your thinking as you do the math!

1 Which man wore the odd-number uniform and which wore the even-number uniform?

_____

_____

2 In one season Gehrig had 49 home runs. How many home runs did he have in the other seasons? Write each number in expanded form to solve the problem.

3 How many of Lou's runs scored in 1927 were not home runs? Write an equation and use mental math to find the number of runs scored that were not home runs.

4 How many more runs did Lou bat in than Babe Ruth one year? Subtract hundreds, tens, and ones to find how many more runs Lou batted in. Check your answer with an addition equation.

NAME _____   DATE _____

Directions: Refer back to the passage and think about this famous baseball player's life. Then, answer the questions below.

1 Why does it say that Lou played in Babe Ruth's shadow? _____

_____

_____

_____

2 Which position did Lou Gehrig play? _____

3 What is Gehrig best known for? _____

_____

_____

_____

4 Why did Lou Gehrig quit playing baseball? _____

_____

_____

_____

5 The end of the passage quotes Lou's teammate. What could you say about Lou Gehrig? Write two or three sentences to describe him.

_____

_____

_____

_____

_____

_____

NAME _____   DATE _____

Wild Winter Weather

Often it's fun to play in the snow. But, sometimes there is too much snow to play in! In the winter of 2014–2015, some cities had a lot of snow. Many storms brought cold weather.

In the Boston area, the snowfall set records. Over 108 inches of snow fell during the winter months. Each storm brought more snow.

Heavy snow began in January. A storm at the end of the month dropped 22 inches. For the whole month, 34 inches of snow fell.

A series of storms came through the area in February. Early in the month, 16 inches of snow fell. This set a record for one day. A week later, another storm added 14 inches. Six days later another storm added 13 inches. Imagine how much snow was on the ground by then! Before the storms in February, 37 inches of snow was already on the ground. It would be hard to build a fort or do anything in that much snow.

THINK ABOUT THE MATH

- Compare the amount on each side of an equation to make sure both sides are equal.
- Use subtraction to find differences in amounts.
- Group by tens to add several numbers together.
- Use mental math for sums and differences already learned.
- Use place-value strategies to add and subtract two- and three-digit numbers.
- Use mental math when an unknown quantity is a multiple of ten.

NAME _____   DATE _____

Directions: Use page 49 to answer these questions. First, skim the paragraphs to find information that might help you solve the problem. Remember to show your thinking as you do the math!

1 How much snow fell during the month of January? _____

How much of the January snow fell in one storm? _____

How much of the snow fell at other times during the month? Write an equation or use a number line to find the difference.

```



```

2 What was the snowfall record for one day? _____

The old record for that date was 11 inches. How much more snow fell on the record day? Use mental math to find the difference.

_____

3 What was the total snowfall for the winter? _____

4 The total snowfall for February was 64 inches. How much snow fell in January and February? Use place-value strategies to find the total amount.

_____

Which strategy did you use? Why did you choose that strategy? Explain how you used the strategy to solve the problem.

_____

_____

5 How much of the record snowfall for the winter did NOT fall during January and February? Write an equation or use mental math to find the answer.

```



```

NAME _____   DATE _____

> **Engage**   **Directions:** Describe the weather you read about and the weather where you live by answering the questions below.

1 Which city did you read about? _____

2 What happened in the winter of 2014–2015? _____

_____

3 What is winter weather like where you live? _____

_____

_____

_____

4 How is it different from the weather you read about? _____

_____

_____

_____

5 What problems might people face in this much snow? _____

_____

_____

_____

_____

6 How does the weather affect people where you live? _____

_____

_____

_____

_____

NAME _____   DATE _____

Small Town U.S.A.: Port Aransas

What would it be like to live on an island? Some islands in our country have towns. Port Aransas is in the Gulf of Mexico. It is part of Texas. The town is on a long barrier island called Mustang Island. The island is 18 miles long. The town takes up 8 miles of it. A barrier island protects the coast from strong storm waves. Storms have destroyed docks and buildings in the town more than once.

The town has changed names several times. Natives first lived there. Later, pirates roamed the area. A legend says there is a chest of gold and jewels buried on the island. People say a Spanish dagger marks the spot. A fort was there during the Civil War.

Fishing has always been important in the town. Over 600 kinds of fish and other sea animals live in the water. At one time, people sold sea turtles for their meat. Several types live in the Gulf waters. The smallest weigh about 100 pounds. Some grow to be 400 pounds or more! They were shipped live on their backs to market. Now people try to save the turtles.

How do people get on and off the island? They drive on a state highway to get to Harbor Island. But there is no bridge across the Corpus Christi channel. A ferry carries people and cars across the water to Port Aransas. Two new boats now carry 28 cars each. The smaller boats carry 20 cars each. The fleet has 8 boats in all.

People also get to the town on a road to the south. It crosses a bridge across a lagoon. They land on another island that has a road that goes to Port Aransas.

NAME _____

DATE _____

Directions: Use page 52 to answer these questions. First, skim the paragraphs to find information that might help you solve the problem. Remember to show your thinking as you do the math!

1 How long is the town? _____   How long is the island? _____

How much of the island is not part of the town? Write an equation to find the unknown number.

```



```

2 How many kinds of fish and other sea animals live in the water?

_____

3 There are 450 species found off the coast of Los Angeles. Use symbols (<, =, or >) to compare the number of types of fish in these two places.

```

```

Which place has more species of fish? _____

4 How many more species of fish are there? Write an equation to find the unknown number.

```

```

5 What is the difference in weight between the types of turtles in the Gulf?

Largest: _____   Smallest: _____

Write an equation to find the difference.

```



```

NAME _____   DATE _____

Engage   **Directions:** Read about ferryboats. Then, answer the questions below.

1 How many boats did the town have before they added the new boats? _____

2 How many total cars can the two new boats carry? _____

3 How many cars can one of the smaller boats carry? _____

If one large boat and two small boats are running today, how many cars can cross the channel at one time? Add multiples of ten to find the total number of cars.

4 Do these ferryboats carry an odd or an even number of cars? _____

5 Draw pictures to show the total number of ferryboats and the cars they carry.

6 How is your picture like an array?

_____

_____

NAME _____   DATE _____

Forest Giants

Giant redwood trees grow in northern California. They need the moist air of the coast to live. The fog traps the moist air in the soil. The trees grow along a narrow strip of land. Their perfect environment is 450 miles long. It is less than 35 miles wide. This area gets about 70 inches of rain per year. Summers are dry. The fog provides moisture to the trees in the summer.

Coast redwoods have the name "giant" for a reason. The largest tree stands 364 feet tall. Its trunk measures 30 feet around. The bark can grow 12 inches thick. Some branches grow up to 5 feet around. It takes a long time for trees to grow this large. Giant redwoods live over 2,000 years.

It is easy to get redwood and sequoia trees mixed up. Sequoia trees grow up to 275 feet. The trunk can be 40 feet around. One large tree grew 310 feet tall. The oldest tree is over 3,000 years old.

The wind carries seeds from the parent tree. The seeds travel only 200 to 400 feet away. Seedlings need lots of water to grow. Once they get started, they grow up to 18 inches in the first year. Trees less than 10 years old may grow over 6 feet in one growing season. New trees also grow from sprouts. These young trees can grow as much as 7 feet in one growing season.

The redwood forest is like a different world. Imagine walking through a grove of huge trees that reach to the sky!

THINK ABOUT THE MATH

- The three digits of a three-digit number represent amounts of hundreds, tens, and ones. The number in the left column of a three-digit number shows how many groups of one hundred are in the amount.
- Ten groups of 100 equals one thousand. We write one thousand as 1,000.
- Think about the number of hundreds, tens, and ones to compare three-digit numbers.
- To add or subtract three-digit numbers, add or subtract hundreds and hundreds, tens and tens, ones and ones.
- Put together or take apart numbers to make tens or hundreds to add or subtract three-digit numbers.
- Use the symbols <, =, and > to compare two numbers.
- Use place-value strategies to add and subtract two- and three-digit numbers.
- Use a number line as a visual model to count by hundreds.
- Use expanded form to compare three-digit numbers.

NAME _____   DATE _____

Problem Solving   **Directions:** Use page 55 to answer these questions. First, skim the paragraphs to find information that might help you solve the problem. Remember to show your thinking as you do the math!

1 Two common trees are maple and pine. Red maple trees rarely live longer than 100 years. Pine trees live 100 years or more. How much longer does the giant redwood tree live? Use a number line or count by 100s to find the answer.

[ ]

2 Some maple trees grow 60 feet tall. Tall maple trees are 90 feet tall. Pine trees are about 100 feet tall. How would you compare the heights of these trees? Write three equations to show the differences in height between two maple trees, between a tall maple tree and a pine tree, and between a maple tree (not tall) and a pine tree.

[ ]

3 How tall is the tallest redwood? _____   How tall is the tallest sequoia? _____

Write each height in expanded form. Use a <, =, or > symbol to compare the heights of the two trees. Which tree is taller?

[ ]

4 How much greater around is the trunk of a sequoia tree than a redwood tree? Write an addition or subtraction equation with an unknown number to show your thinking.

[ ]

5 Giant redwoods live _____ years. The oldest sequoia is over _____ years old.

What is the difference in age between the redwood and the sequoia? _____

Explain how you used place value to find the difference. _____

_____

_____

NAME _____   DATE _____

Directions: A model is a small picture of something large. Think about ways you can draw and describe these forest giants. Then, answer the questions below.

1 What is another unit of measurement you could use to describe the thickness of redwood bark? Draw a picture or write a true number statement.

2 This page is not big enough to draw a tree as its real size. What smaller unit of measurement can you use to draw this tree?

_____

3 Draw a picture or visual model to compare the heights of maple, pine, sequoia, and redwood trees side by side.

Which tree is the shortest? _____

Which trees are closest in height? _____

NAME _____   DATE _____

Cyrus McCormick: Help for Farmers

Long ago, farmers cut grain by hand. It took a long time to harvest, so they could not plant large crops. A man named Cyrus wanted to change that. His father worked to make a machine that would cut grain. He worked for 16 years but was not successful. Cyrus took over his father's work in 1831, and in 6 weeks he had a working machine. Horses pulled the reaper through the field. It cut, threshed, and bundled the grain. He took out a patent in 1834.

Cyrus moved to the Midwest in 1848 and opened a factory. The first year his factory made 500 reapers. Three years later it made 1,000 machines. The business kept growing. Cyrus made his machines better each year. He wanted to help farmers so he gave them credit. Farmers could use the machine and pay when they sold their crops. Cyrus worked hard his whole life until he died in 1884.

NAME _____   DATE _____

Directions: Use page 58 to answer these questions. First, skim the paragraphs to find information that might help you solve the problem. Remember to show your thinking as you do the math!

1 How long did Cyrus's father work to make a reaper? _____

How long after that did Cyrus work on the machine? _____

Who worked longer on the invention, the father or the son? _____

Use a <, =, or > symbol to write a true number sentence to show your answer.

2 How many reapers did the factory make the first year? _____

How many did it make 3 years later? _____

How many more machines did they make in 1851 than in 1848? _____

3 Cyrus was 22 when he took over his father's work. In what year was he born? Write an equation or use a number line to show your work.

4 How long did Cyrus live? Write an equation or group by tens and hundreds to find the number of years Cyrus lived.

How did you find the answer to this question? Explain. _____

_____

_____

_____

NAME _____   DATE _____

1 In what year did Cyrus's father start working on a reaper? Write an equation to show your thinking.

2 How many years after he made a working reaper did Cyrus take out a patent? Write an equation to show your thinking.

3 How old was Cyrus when he started his factory? Write an equation to show your thinking.

4 In what year did the factory make 1,000 reapers? Write an equation to show your thinking.

5 What did it mean for Cyrus to give the farmers credit? Explain. _____

_____

_____

NAME _____   DATE _____

Flying in the Wind

It's a sunny day with a breeze in the meadow. This is great weather to fly a kite! It takes string to fly a kite. Kite string comes in different lengths. They are used for different kinds of kites.

Stunt kites have lines as short as 50 feet. This allows the kite to make quick, short turns. People who have experience use this string. Someone who is new to stunt kites will use a longer line. It might be as long as 100 feet. The kite will make slower turns. This makes it easier to control.

Power kites give kite fliers a range of experiences. Small kites tug and dance in the winds. Huge power kites pull people. These people can ride surfboards, wind boards, or skateboards. Power kites need lines at least 75 feet long. Some need 100-foot lines. The amount of line needed depends on the wind. Kites might have a single line or two lines. Some kites have as many as 4 lines.

A tail keeps the kite stable. If the tail is too long, it makes the kite heavy. It will not fly as well. The tail should be 8 times as long as the kite. Attach the tail and watch a kite soar!

THINK ABOUT THE MATH

- Use measurement tools to measure and draw the length of objects.

- Centimeters are a smaller measurement unit than inches.

- There are 12 inches in one foot.

- There are 3 feet in one yard.

- Group by tens to estimate lengths in inches.

- Use a number line to represent lengths of objects.

- Use mental math to add or subtract multiples of ten.

- Draw pictures to show what is happening in a problem.

- Draw an array to find the total number in equal-sized groups.

NAME _____   DATE _____

Directions: Use page 61 to answer these questions. First, skim the paragraphs to find information that might help you solve the problem. Remember to show your thinking as you do the math!

1 What is the difference in length between the shortest and the longest stunt kite lines?

_____

2 What is the difference between the shortest stunt kite line and the shortest power kite line?

_____

3 About how many inches are in a short stunt kite line? Group by tens and hundreds. Use a number line to estimate the length in inches.

4 If a stunt kite has 4 lines, what is the least amount of kite string you need?

_____

5 If a power kite has 2 lines, how much kite string do you need?

_____

6 If the kite is 3 feet long, how long a tail does it need? Use a number line or draw an array to find the length of the tail.

NAME _____ DATE _____

Engage **Directions:** Draw a model of a kite. Use your drawing to answer the questions below.

1 What type of kite did you draw? _____

2 Draw a line and a tail for your kite.

3 What measurement unit would be best to use to measure your model drawing: centimeters, inches, feet, or yards? _____

How much line does your kite need? Measure it. _____

4 How does your kite compare to a classmate's? Which kite is smaller?

_____

_____

Which kite has a longer tail? _____

What is the length of string on each kite? _____

What is the difference between the lengths of string? _____

NAME _____ DATE _____

Rapunzel

Once upon a time, a woman was about to have a child. She saw some greens in the neighbor's garden. Her husband agreed to get them for her. A witch owned the garden. The husband crept over the wall at twilight to get the rapunzel. There stood the angry witch. "How dare you come and steal my rapunzel? You will suffer!"

He explained, and the witch said, "You may take as many greens as you want, but you must give me your child when it is born. I will care for it as a mother." The witch came at the baby's birth to take it away. She named the child Rapunzel.

Rapunzel grew to be very beautiful. When she was twelve, the witch shut her in a tower that had no stairs or door. When the witch came to visit, she stood below the window. "Rapunzel, Rapunzel, let down your hair to me."

Rapunzel's hair was very long, fine as spun gold. She undid her braids and let her hair fall thirty feet out the window. The witch climbed up her hair.

A year or two later, the king's son rode through the forest. He passed the tower and heard Rapunzel singing. But he did not see a door to the tower. He came back every day to listen. One day, he stood behind a tree. He saw the witch and heard her call to Rapunzel.

The next day, he went to the tower and said the words. When the hair fell down, he climbed up. Rapunzel was frightened when a man appeared. He talked kindly to her, and she agreed to go away with him. First they had to find a way to get her out of the tower. "Bring a skein of silk every time you come," she said. "I will weave a ladder with it."

The king's son came at night since the witch came during the day. One day, Rapunzel remarked that the witch was much heavier for her to pull up than the king's son. In her anger, the witch cut Rapunzel's hair. She took the girl to the desert to live. The witch kept the braids and hung them from the window.

When the king's son learned Rapunzel was gone, he leapt from the tower. He escaped alive but fell into thorns. They pierced his eyes and made him blind. He wandered for many years and at last came to the desert. He heard a familiar voice. Rapunzel wet his eyes with her tears and, as a result, the king's son could see again. They returned to his home and lived happily ever after.

NAME _____   DATE _____

Problem Solving   **Directions:** Use page 64 to answer these questions. First, skim the paragraphs to find information that might help you solve the problem. Remember to show your thinking as you do the math!

1 Draw a picture of the tower. Label the tower to show how tall it is.

2 How far did Rapunzel let down her hair? _____

3 How many feet are in a yard? _____

How many yards is thirty feet? _____

4 What other measurement is close to a yard? _____

About how many meters tall was Rapunzel's tower? _____

5 How many centimeters are in a meter? _____

About how many centimeters tall was Rapunzel's tower? Use a number line to solve the problem.

6 One story of a building is about 10 feet. How many stories is a tower that is thirty feet tall?

_____

NAME _____   DATE _____

Engage   **Directions:** Refer to the passage and use the information given below to answer the math questions.

1 Most likely, Rapunzel's braids didn't reach quite to the ground. How long do you think her braids were?

_____

2 Let's say Rapunzel was 47 inches tall. Her braids start about 6 inches from the top of her head. If her braids were 36 inches long, would her hair reach the floor?

_____

Write equations to show how many inches there would be between the end of her braids and the ground.

_____

3 Draw a picture of a ladder. How many yards of silk do you think Rapunzel will need to weave a ladder?

_____

4 If the witch cut 24 inches off Rapunzel's braids, how long would her braids be? Use the information in question 2 to write an equation.

_____

NAME _____   DATE _____

Track Meet

Tyler laced up his running shoes. The shoes and his new shorts made him look as though he was part of the track team, even though he was too young. He was looking forward to watching his older brother take part in the track meet today.

On the way, Noah explained the meet. "I run in the 400m dash and do the long jump and high jump. Other people run shorter or longer distances and do other events."

"How fast do you run?" Tyler wanted to know.

Noah bounced his legs as if warming up. "It takes me about a minute and a half to run around the track. I'm better at jumping than running."

As soon as the van stopped, the boys scrambled out. "Show me the long jump," Tyler said. "What do you do?"

"I run down a track and jump into a box of sand. The referees see where my feet land and measure how far I jump." Noah led the way to the jumping area.

"What's that?" Tyler pointed to two vertical poles next to a thick mat. A horizontal bar hung across the poles.

"The high jump."

"I don't think I could jump that high!"

Noah chuckled. "Neither can I. They'll lower the bar when it's time to jump."

"You'll do great!" Tyler gave his brother a high five and then went to find a seat in the stands.

THINK ABOUT THE MATH

- There are 12 inches in one foot.
- There are 60 seconds in one minute.
- Use a number line to create a visual model of what is happening in a problem.
- Group by tens to work with numbers over 100.

NAME _____   DATE _____

Problem Solving   **Directions:** Use page 67 to answer these questions. First, skim the paragraphs to find information that might help you solve the problem. Remember to show your thinking as you do the math!

1 Today, Noah ran his race in 1 minute and 14 seconds.

How long did he think it would take to run the race? _____

How much faster did he run today? _____

How many seconds did it take him to run the entire race? _____

His teammate ran the race in 1 minute and 10 seconds. How much faster was his teammate's time?

_____

Draw a number line if you need help finding the times.

_____

2 For the long jump, Tyler jumped 10 feet 2 inches. How many inches did he jump in all? Group by tens to find the total number of inches.

_____

Tyler's teammate jumped 9 feet 8 inches. How many inches did he jump in all?

_____

3 Which boy jumped the farthest? Draw a part of a number line to show the difference in length the boys jumped. Number it in inches.

_____

Label each boy's jump on the number line.

What is the difference in the distance the boys jumped? _____

Write an equation to show the distance in length.

_____

NAME _____   DATE _____

Engage | **Directions:** Set up a jumping area in your classroom or on the playground. Then, answer the questions below.

1 Take turns with your classmates to see how far you can jump. Use masking tape to mark where your feet land.

How far did you jump from a standing position? _____

How far did you jump from a running start? _____

2 On the lines below, write the distances one or more classmates jumped from either a standing position or a running start.

_____   _____
            Name   Distance

_____   _____
            Name   Distance

_____   _____
            Name   Distance

_____   _____
            Name   Distance

3 Draw a picture of your jumping area. Draw a number line as part of it.

Mark to show the distances you and your classmates jumped.

4 Write equations to show the differences in distances you and your classmates jumped.

NAME _____   DATE _____

Kart Racing

Go-karts look like fun. Other karts are built to race. A kart club might have its own track. Some clubs have races for children or teenagers. It can be a good family sport.

Clubs have rules. The rules help people stay safe. They also make the races fair for everyone.

People race indoors or outdoors. Each type of race has a different kind of track. Some races last longer than others. Sprints are short races. They last 15 minutes or less. Enduro races last from 20 minutes to 45 minutes. These races take place on full-size tracks. The shortest full-size track is one mile long. Tracks can be over two miles long. Sprint tracks are often less than one mile long.

Before a race, racers can practice. People practice by group. A practice time lasts no more than 10 minutes for a weekend race. On other days, racers might have 15 or 20 minutes to practice. Different tracks offer different practice times. The times can change during the day if more karts show up.

Karts reach different speeds in races. On a short track, karts might go 50 miles per hour. On a full-size track, karts can reach speeds up to 100 miles per hour! Some classes of races allow two engines. Imagine how fast those karts might go!

NAME _____   DATE _____

Problem Solving   **Directions:** Use page 70 to answer these questions. First, skim the paragraphs to find information that might help you solve the problem. Remember to show your thinking as you do the math!

1 How many minutes is the longest sprint race? _____

How many minutes is the shortest enduro race? _____

What is the difference between these two races? _____

Draw a picture or write an equation to show how you found the difference between the two times.

2 How many minutes is the longest enduro race? _____

How much longer is this than the shortest enduro race? _____

Write equations or use mental math to find your answer.

3 If the longest sprint race begins at 1:00 p.m., what time will it end? Show the time on both the analog and digital clocks.

4 A long enduro race starts at 2:00 p.m. What time will it end? Show the time on both the analog and digital clocks.

5 How long is the practice time for a weekend race? _____

How long is the practice time during the week? _____

How much longer can racers practice during the week? _____

Use mental math or <, =, or > to compare the practice times.

NAME _____   DATE _____

> **Engage**   **Directions:** Look back at the passage or read more about kart racing to answer the questions below.

1 What two types of races did you read about? _____

_____

What is a sprint race? _____

_____

What is an enduro race? _____

_____

2 How long is a sprint track? _____

How long is a full-size track? _____

3 What makes a difference in how long racers can practice? _____

_____

4 What is the fastest speed in a kart race? _____

Is that faster or slower than the speed of a car driving the speed limit on a freeway?

_____

How much faster or slower do these fast karts go than cars? _____

5 Why might someone want to take part in kart racing? _____

_____

_____

_____

_____

_____

_____

NAME _____   DATE _____

Going to a Market

Many towns have a farmers' market. Often, a street is blocked off. Farmers will come to sell produce one or two days a week. Other vendors may sell things, too. You might find jam made from local berries. Some farmers keep bees and bring fresh honey to sell. A local bakery may bring baked goods. Often, food-cart vendors will sell hot foods. A walk through a farmers' market has many sights and smells.

Farmers bring produce that grows in that area. They grow things they think people will buy. They want their supply to meet the demand. This makes a difference in how much money farmers make. They set their prices based on different things. If apple prices go up, people will probably buy another kind of fruit. Good weather will bring a large apple crop. Prices will go down, and people will buy more apples. Weather affects crops. Prices change from one year to the next. Sometimes it costs farmers more or less to grow different foods.

More people buy fruits and vegetables from small farms now than in the past. Food is not always cheaper at a small market, but some people think the produce is healthier. People who shop at a farmers' market want to help support local farms.

The chart below compares prices in 2008 and 2013.

Food	2008 price	2013 price
apples	$1.07 / pound	$1.57 / pound
grapes	$1.68 / pound	$2.09 / pound
oranges	57¢ / pound	$1.04 / pound
pears	$1.04 / pound	$1.46 / pound
carrots	77¢ / pound	74¢ / pound
green beans	$3.23 / pound	$2.14 / pound
green peppers	$2.13 / pound	$1.41 / pound
tomatoes	$2.94 / pound	$1.24 / pound

THINK ABOUT THE MATH

- A penny is worth one cent.
- A nickel is worth five cents.
- A dime is worth ten cents.
- A quarter is worth twenty-five cents.
- A dollar is worth one hundred cents.
- The $ symbol is used to show the number of dollars.
- The ¢ symbol is used to show the number of cents.
- Use a letter in place of an unknown number in an equation.
- Write equations to represent what is happening in a problem.
- Use place-value strategies such as counting on, making a group of ten, or breaking apart a group of ten to add and subtract two-digit numbers.

NAME _____   DATE _____

Problem Solving

Directions: Use page 73 to answer these questions. First, skim the paragraphs to find information that might help you solve the problem. Remember to show your thinking as you do the math!

1 In 2013, which food costs less than $1.00 per pound? _____

2 Which food(s) went down in price? _____

_____

_____

What do these foods all have in common? _____

3 Why might the prices have gone down? _____

_____

_____

_____

4 What is the difference in the price of apples? _____

What is the difference in the price of oranges? _____

What is another way to write 57¢? _____

5 Which fruit went up more in price, apples or oranges? _____

How much more did that price go up? _____

6 Write one or two math questions based on what you read in the chart and solve them.

_____

_____

_____

_____

_____

NAME _____   DATE _____

> **Engage** | **Directions:** Read the passage. Then, answer the questions below.

1 What are some things people sell at a farmers' market? _____

_____

_____

_____

2 How many days a week can you go to the farmers' market? _____

_____

_____

_____

3 How do farmers decide what to grow and sell? _____

_____

_____

_____

4 What happens if the price goes up on one kind of fruit? _____

_____

_____

_____

5 What are some things that affect food prices? _____

_____

_____

_____

6 Why do people shop at farmers' markets? _____

_____

_____

_____

NAME _____   DATE _____

A Different Kind of Pet

They're not a pet you can hold or take for a walk. But, some people keep fish as pets. They keep fish in a tank, or aquarium. Some tanks have warm water, and some have colder water. Some are filled with fresh water, while others are filled with salt water. Aquarium fish come in many colors and sizes. Some fish do well with other kinds of fish, and some do not. It's important to know which fish get along well before setting up a tank.

The size of tank limits the number of fish. A general rule is one inch of fish for every gallon of water. Know the size the fish will grow to. Fish may be smaller to start. Some tanks have rocks and plants. They do not hold as many gallons of water for fish to swim.

Some fish are tiny. Tetras are less than 2 inches long. Guppies and zebra danios grow to 2 or $2\frac{1}{2}$ inches. Penguinfish look like their name. They have a black stripe down their side and grow to about 3 inches. Black mollies also reach a length of 3 inches. The size of goldfish depends on where they live. They can be as small as 2 or 3 inches. In a pond, they grow much larger.

Other fish are even bigger. If there are many in a fish tank, it needs to be large. Angelfish grow up to 8 inches. They are a tall fish with big fins. Sun catfish grow to 8 or 10 inches. The clown loach isn't quite as big. It grows to about 7 inches. The oscar surprises people. It starts out small but can grow as large as 14 inches!

NAME _____   DATE _____

Problem Solving   **Directions:** Use page 76 to answer these questions. First, skim the paragraphs to find information that might help you solve the problem. Remember to show your thinking as you do the math!

1 What unit of measurement is used to measure fish for a fish tank? _____

2 What is the smallest length of fish mentioned? _____

3 What is the longest fish mentioned? _____

4 Which fish are longer than the clown loach? _____

_____

5 Which fish has a size based on where it lives? _____

6 Draw a line plot. Mark it in whole number units to match the maximum lengths of fish in the reading passage. Draw an X or dot for each fish above the mark on the number line that shows the length of that fish.

NAME _____   DATE _____

Engage   **Directions:** Use the information in the passage to complete the activity below.

1 Draw a picture graph. Draw pictures to show the number of fish in each category.

[blank box]

Fish less than 5 inches in length: _____

_____

Fish 5 to 10 inches in length: _____

_____

Fish more than 10 inches in length: _____

_____

2 How many fish are 10 inches long or smaller? _____

3 How many fish are over 5 inches in length? _____

4 How many more fish are under 5 inches in length than over 5 inches? _____

5 How many fish are shown on this graph in all? _____

NAME _____   DATE _____

Lighthouses

Have you ever wondered how ships find their way at night or in the fog? Sometimes the coast is rocky with cliffs. Ships need to stay safe. A lighthouse is a tower with a light on top. In foggy areas, a warning sounds.

Lighthouses also guide ships by marking an important place. For example, there might be a lighthouse next to a channel. There are over 700 lighthouses in the United States. They are along both ocean coasts. There are also some on the Gulf of Mexico and the Great Lakes.

Not all lighthouses are the same shape. In a flat area, it might be tall. On a high rocky cliff, a lighthouse might be short. One on the East Coast has an octagon shape. Another lighthouse has a hexagon shape. Others are shaped like a cone. Some have a cylinder shape. They are also made of different materials. People used whatever was handy: stone, wood, or brick. Some are made of a mixture of shells, lime, sand, and water called *tabby*.

Sailors identify lighthouses by their color and shape. Lighthouses are painted with different colors and patterns. They are different shapes. Each lighthouse also has a different flashing pattern for the light. The light turns, and it looks like it flashes on and off. Sailors look at a chart to find the pattern. Then they know where they are along the coast.

THINK ABOUT THE MATH

- An angle is a figure formed by two lines that start at the same point.
- A face is any of the individual surfaces of a solid shape.
- A square or rectangle has four sides and four right angles.
- An octagon is an eight-sided, closed shape. It has eight angles.
- A hexagon is a six-sided, closed shape. It has six angles.
- A cylinder has two same-sized round, flat faces and a curved side that connects them.
- A cone is a shape with a round base and a point at the top.
- Count the number of angles and faces to identify a shape.

NAME _____   DATE _____

Directions: Use page 79 to answer these questions. First, skim the paragraphs to find information that might help you solve the problem. Remember to show your thinking as you do the math!

1 What are two unusual shapes of lighthouses?

_____

How many sides or angles does each have?

_____

Draw pictures of these lighthouses and label each.

2 What do we call the shape of a lighthouse that looks like a tall pipe?

_____

Draw a picture of this kind of lighthouse.

3 What shape is a lighthouse that is round and wider at the base and narrow on top?

_____

Draw a picture of this kind of lighthouse.

4 Color your drawings with different colors and patterns to tell them apart.

NAME _____   DATE _____

Engage   **Directions:** Use the chart below to write math problems about lighthouses to share with classmates.
For example, which lighthouse is the tallest? How much taller is it than _____?

Name of Lighthouse	State	Height	Type of Tower	Unusual Facts
Whitehead Island	Maine	41 ft.	stone tower	
Statue of Liberty	New York	305 ft.	sculpture	torch served as a beacon until 1902
St. Augustine	Florida	165 ft.	black-and-white painted, spiral tower	
Boston	Massachusetts	89 ft.	white, round, stone tower	first light station 1716
Cape Hatteras	North Carolina	210 ft.	black-and-white painted, round, brick tower on a red brick, octagon base	tallest brick lighthouse
Forty Mile Point	Michigan	52 ft.	square, brick tower	on Lake Huron
Los Angeles Harbor	California	69 ft.	steel and concrete, cylinder tower	
Alcatraz Island	California	84 ft.	unpainted, octagon, concrete tower	first West Coast light station

Tip: Read library books or look at websites to learn more about lighthouses.

_____

_____

_____

_____

_____

_____

NAME _____   DATE _____

Sandcastle Fun

"Can we go to the beach, Grandpa?" Ella hopped into the living room in stocking feet. "We want to build a sandcastle."

"Find some things to use to make your castle and put your shoes on." Grandpa went in search of his flip-flops.

Ella wandered into the kitchen. "What can we use, Grandma?"

Grandma handed her a funnel and a round container. She handed Kate some spoons and an empty plastic sandwich box.

Kate and Ella scampered ahead of Grandpa on the narrow wooded path to the beach. As soon as they reached the sand, Kate began searching for sticks. Ella ran ahead and then stopped.

"Here. This is a good flat place."

Grandpa looked around. "The tide won't come this far for hours. I'll sit on this log and watch you."

Ella smoothed the sand. Next to the flat place, she filled the sandwich box with sand and dumped it to form part of the walls. She added round shapes at each corner of the castle using the round container. Kate joined her and used the funnel to add towers to the walls.

After they had built awhile, Kate picked up a stick. She drew patterns in the sand.

"What are those?" Ella pointed.

Kate pointed to a pentagon drawn in the sand. "This is where the drawbridge rests when it's down." She moved the stick to drawings of hexagons in the sand. "And these are places for knights to stand when they practice throwing javelins."

"I see. We'd better go find some figures to live and play at the castle." Ella skipped down the beach in search of small wood pieces.

NAME _____   DATE _____

Directions: Use page 82 to answer these questions. First, skim the paragraphs to find information that might help you solve the problem. Remember to show your thinking as you do the math!

1 What shape were the objects Grandma handed Ella and Kate? Write the shape names under the pictures.

_____   _____   _____

What is true of each of these shapes? _____

_____

_____

_____

2 Which shape did Ella use for the walls of the castle? _____

Which shape did Kate use for the towers on the walls? _____

3 Where did Ella put cylinder shapes? _____

4 Why did Kate draw a pentagon?

_____

Draw a picture to show the shape of the drawbridge.

5 Draw the place where the knights would practice throwing the javelin.

What shape is it?

_____

NAME _____   DATE _____

1 Label the shapes in your drawing.

2 Describe your sandcastle. Use the names of shapes to describe parts of your castle.

_____

_____

_____

_____

NAME _____   DATE _____

Energy from the Sun

Some people think they have more energy on sunny days. Plants get energy from the sun. Animals eat plants, and their food gives them energy. We eat plants and animals, and our food gives us energy.

The sun gives off energy. A lot of this energy does not get used. It does not cause pollution. More and more, we use solar energy for power.

A solar panel captures the sun's energy. The panel has many cells. Each cell has matter that conducts electricity. When the sunlight hits the cells, it knocks things in the cells loose. These things make electricity as they move around the cell.

Small solar cells work together on a solar panel. Together they make enough power to be useful. Solar panels face the sun. This way they get the most energy possible. Calculators use small solar panels. A solar panel on the rooftop of a home heats or cools the house and provides hot water. Large solar panels make electricity for buildings. They are also on the roof. Huge solar farms make power for many houses and offices. They take up a lot of land.

THINK ABOUT THE MATH

- A rectangle can be divided into rows and columns of same-size squares.
- A rectangle divided into rows and columns looks like an array.
- An array is an arrangement of objects in a number of equal-sized rows.
- Draw an array to count how many total objects are in a set of equal-sized groups.
- Think about multiples of tens or group by tens to divide a total amount into a number of equal-sized rows.

NAME _____   DATE _____

Problem Solving

Directions: Use page 85 to answer these questions. First, skim the paragraphs to find information that might help you solve the problem. Remember to show your thinking as you do the math!

1 What shape is a solar panel? _____

2 What makes up a solar panel? _____

3 How would you describe the solar panels on page 85? _____

_____

_____

4 How many solar cells are on this solar panel?

_____

5 Draw a house roof with a solar panel on it. The panel should have 60 cells.

```



```

How many rows are in your panel? _____

How many cells are in each row? _____

NAME _____   DATE _____

1 Where do solar panels get energy from? _____

2 Which side of a house or building are solar panels on? _____

_____

3 How would you design the cells on a solar panel to make the best use of space?

_____

_____

4 Where have you seen solar panels? _____

_____

_____

_____

_____

_____

_____

5 Where in your town could solar panels be used? _____

_____

_____

_____

_____

_____

_____

NAME _____   DATE _____

City Blocks

Why do some towns have straight streets? A long time ago, people moved west. They moved from cities to open land. As people settled in the West, they drew maps. A township was a square that was 6 miles on each side. Each township had 36 sections. A section was 1 mile on each side. Each section was divided into four parcels. A quarter section was called a *homestead*.

During this time, when people wanted to move west, the government would give them free land. If a person lived on the land for 5 years, the homestead would be theirs. People had to build a house and farm during the 5 years. At the end of that time, they could pay a fee of $18 to own the land.

The lines between sections became roads. The roads were one mile apart. Streets were laid along these lines. As townships grew, they divided the one-mile sections into quarters. These were divided into fourths again. From there, different cities divided blocks in different ways. Now towns have city blocks shaped like squares or rectangles.

NAME _____ DATE _____

Problem Solving | **Directions:** Use page 88 to answer these questions. First, skim the paragraphs to find information that might help you solve the problem. Remember to show your thinking as you do the math!

1 Draw a square to show the size of a township. Label the number of miles on each side.

2 How many sections was a township divided into? _____

Draw lines on your township square to show the sections.

3 If each section is 1 mile wide, how many sections are in each row? _____

If each section is 1 mile long, how many rows are in a township? _____

Draw an array to show 36 sections.

4 How many parcels were in one section? _____

How much of a section is one homestead? _____

5 Draw a homestead. Label its sides. Divide it into quarters. Use a different color pencil to divide each quarter into fourths. How many parcels do you have now?

_____

NAME _____   DATE _____

Engage | **Directions:** Use the information in the passage and your own ideas to plan and draw a town. Share your plans with classmates.

---

1 How many homesteads have been settled in your town? Outline those with a dark pencil.

2 Are some sections divided into smaller parcels?

3 Where will you put roads?

4 Which parcels will have businesses?

5 Which community buildings, such as schools or libraries, will you include?

NAME _____   DATE _____

The World of Soccer

Soccer is played by people in many countries. The game is played on a field in the shape of a rectangle. The field has end lines and sidelines. These lines form the boundaries. If a ball is kicked past these lines, it is out of bounds and the other team gets the ball.

At each end of the field, a box is marked. A net stands at the edge of the box. Players kick the ball into the net. This is the goal box. One player tries to keep the ball out of the net. That player is the goalie. When a team kicks the ball into the net, they score a point. A larger box might be marked outside the goal box. It is a penalty box. In this area, goalies can touch the ball with their hands. The penalty arc is where a player stands to take a penalty kick. This is awarded when someone from the other team makes a foul in their penalty area.

In each corner of the field are quarter circles called corner arcs. Sometimes a player will make a corner kick. This happens when the ball goes out of bounds at the end line. The ball is placed inside the arc, and the player kicks it.

A line is drawn across the center of the field. This divides the field into two parts. Each team defends one part. The center line is called the halfway line. The game starts within a circle on the halfway line.

THINK ABOUT THE MATH

- A circle is a closed shape with no straight lines.
- A rectangle is a closed shape with four straight sides. It has four right angles.
- Circles and rectangles can be divided into two, three, or four equal parts.
- Equal parts of identical wholes do not need to have the same shape.
- Count the angles to draw named shapes.
- Draw lines to divide shapes into two or four equal parts.
- Look at a diagram to draw a picture of what the text describes.

NAME _____   DATE _____

Directions: Use page 91 to answer these questions. First, skim the paragraphs to find information that might help you solve the problem. Remember to show your thinking as you do the math!

1 Draw a rectangle. Divide it into two equal parts. What is each part called?

_____

Which parts of a soccer field are a half-rectangle shape?

_____

2 Draw a rectangle. Divide it into four equal parts. What is each part called?

_____

Which parts of a soccer field are a quarter-rectangle shape?

_____

3 Draw a circle. Divide it into two equal parts. What is each part called?

_____

Which part of a soccer field is a half-circle shape?

_____

4 Draw a circle. Divide it into four equal parts. What is each part called?

_____

Which parts of a soccer field are a quarter-circle shape?

_____

NAME _____   DATE _____

1 What happens in the center circle? _____

_____

_____

_____

2 Who stands in the goal box in front of the net? _____

3 Which part of the field is within another area of the field? _____

_____

_____

_____

4 What happens in the penalty box? _____

_____

_____

_____

_____

_____

5 What happens in the quarter circles at the corners of the field? _____

_____

_____

_____

_____

_____

_____

NAME _____ DATE _____

Tasty Cornbread

Native people grew corn as a main part of their diet. They dried the corn and ground it into meal. The meal was made into cakes or bread. Natives baked the cakes on hot rocks. Settlers used round iron pans. At first it was called "hoe cake" because they could bake a small cake on a garden hoe. People ate the bread with soup or stew.

People ate cornbread often. They used things they had on hand, such as cornmeal, water, and cooking fat. They added salt if they had it. Native people may have added seeds, nuts, or berries.

As time went on, settlers added other things to the bread. They had cows and chickens on a farm. This meant they could use milk, butter, and eggs. Maple trees and bees provided sugar and honey. Yeast or baking soda made the bread rise.

In the north, cornbread became a light, sweet bread. People mixed flour with the cornmeal. They added honey or molasses to the bread. In the south, cornbread wasn't as sweet. Today, there are many different recipes for cornbread.

NAME _____   DATE _____

Problem Solving | **Directions:** Use page 94 to answer these questions. First, skim the paragraphs to find information that might help you solve the problem. Remember to show your thinking as you do the math!

1 In what shape might people form cornbread with their hands to bake on rocks or a flat metal hoe?

_____

2 What shape pan did settlers use to bake cornbread? _____

3 In the space below, draw a picture of cornbread in a rectangular pan. Measure and draw the pan 6 inches across. Draw lines to divide it into pieces. How many equal parts did you divide it into? _____

4 If a pioneer woman has a husband and two sons, into how many pieces will she cut their cornbread? Draw lines in the circle to show this so that they all have one piece.

_____

5 How much of the cornbread will her sons eat in all?

_____

Shade the circle to show how much cornbread they will eat.

6 How much cornbread will the woman eat? Draw lines on her piece to show how much she will eat.

_____

NAME _____   DATE _____

Directions: Discuss with classmates your experiences with cornbread. Then, answer the questions below.

1 Why was cornbread called "hoe cake" a long time ago? _____

_____

_____

2 Why has cornbread been a common food for many years? _____

_____

_____

_____

3 What are things people have added to cornbread over the years? _____

_____

_____

_____

4 If you have had cornbread, what is your favorite way to eat it? If you have not had cornbread, how do you think you would like to try it?

_____

_____

_____

_____

NAME _____   DATE _____

Movie Day

Alana spread the blanket out and smoothed the corners with her hands. "Is the popcorn ready?" She poked her head into the kitchen.

Cody set three bowls on the counter. "Yes, Mom just finished making it."

"We'll each have a third of the popcorn." Nolan picked up two bowls and carried them into the living room. Cody followed with the other bowl.

"We can divide the blanket, too," Alana said. She turned to Cody's mom. "Do you have string or yarn?"

Alana took the pieces of yarn and arranged them on the blanket. She pointed to the middle of the blanket. "Nolan, you can sit there."

He set his bowl of popcorn on the blanket and stood by Cody to look at movies in the bookshelf.

"Can we watch this one, Mom?" Cody handed her a movie.

"Careful!" Alana watched as Cody made a flying leap to the blanket, popcorn in hand.

> **THINK ABOUT THE MATH**
>
> - A rectangle can be divided into three equal parts or shares.
> - Each part is called a *third*.
> - There are three thirds in a whole.
> - A rectangle can be divided into equal parts in many different ways.
> - Use objects to create a visual model to understand ways to divide shapes into equal shares.
> - Draw a picture to show what is happening in a problem.

NAME _____   DATE _____

Directions: Use page 97 to answer these questions. First, skim the paragraphs to find information that might help you solve the problem. Remember to show your thinking as you do the math!

1 How many children will sit on the blanket? _____

How did Alana divide the blanket? _____

What is each area called? _____

Draw a picture of
the blanket with
the children sitting
on it.

2 How many equal shares did Mom divide the popcorn into? _____

What is each share called? _____

Draw a picture of the popcorn bowls.

3 Why did Alana divide the blanket into different areas? _____

_____

4 How many bowls of popcorn would they need if Mom had some popcorn? _____

How much popcorn would each person have? _____

Draw a circle to represent the bowl of
popcorn. Divide it into equal shares
for the four of them.

NAME _____   DATE _____

1 Draw a picture of your model.

What shape is your area? _____

2 How much of the area will be for you? _____ Shade that part of your drawing.

3 How much of the area will be for your classmates? _____ Use a different color to shade that part on your drawing.

4 Rearrange your model to include another person.

How many parts is your area divided into now? _____

Draw a picture of your changed model.

5 How much of the area do you have? _____

NAME _____   DATE _____

George Washington Carver: Not Just Peanut Butter

George Washington Carver grew up in the South. He was a slave. After the Civil War, slavery ended. His former masters taught him to read and write. George went on to college. He wanted to help farmers. He taught them about crop rotation. Each crop gets its food from the soil. When farmers grew the same thing each year, the soil became poor. George Carver told farmers to grow crops in different places each year to preserve the soil.

Many farmers in the South grew cotton. An insect often ate cotton crops. The insect didn't like peanuts. Farmers needed to grow things they could sell to make money. They didn't think they could make enough money growing peanuts. George Carver invented things. He used peanuts, sweet potatoes, and soy beans in some of his inventions.

This convinced farmers to grow these crops. He made cooking oil and dyes for clothing from peanuts. He used peanuts to make plastic. He did not invent peanut butter, but he did make his own. Did you know it takes 500 peanuts to make 1 jar of peanut butter? Imagine what else a person could do with peanuts.

NAME _____   DATE _____

Directions: Use page 100 to answer these questions. First, skim the paragraphs to find information that might help you solve the problem. Remember to show your thinking as you do the math!

1 How would you describe the general shape of a peanut? _____

2 What shape is a jar of peanut butter? What attributes does it have? _____

_____

_____

3 What other foods come in this shape? _____

_____

_____

4 Draw a farm.

_____

Divide your farm in half. Divide one half into quarters. What crops could a farmer grow? Write the name of a crop in each field.

Now a year has gone by. Draw the farm again. You want to grow the same crops. But George Washington Carver says not to put them in the same places. Where will you plant each crop this time? Label the fields in your farm.

_____

NAME _____   DATE _____

1 What was one way George helped farmers? _____

_____

_____

_____

2 What does it mean to **rotate** crops? _____

_____

_____

_____

3 What crop were the farmers growing? _____

Why did farmers need to find other crops to grow? _____

_____

_____

_____

4 What other crops did George Washington Carver tell them about? _____

_____

_____

_____

5 What are some things he made from peanuts? _____

_____

_____

_____

Answer Key

The Blue Angels (pages 7–9)

Problem Solving: 1. 6; even 2. 2 3. $16 - 8 = 8$
4. even; Students might draw planes in pairs to show there are no extra left over. 5. other officers; 3 years officers > 2 years pilots 6. $700 - 120 = 580$ miles per hour

Engage: 1. a team of pilots and officers from the Navy and Marines 2. put on air shows and talk to people in communities around the country 3. *Suggested answer:* to entertain people, to help people understand what the military does, to show people how fighter pilots fly 4. diamond 5. 18 in.; Answers will vary; it's one-and-a-half ruler lengths.

A Day at the Playground (pages 10–12)

Problem Solving: 1. They have the same number.
2. odd; There will be one left over if counted by 2s; 13 bars on each ladder 3.–4. Answers will vary.
5. $47 + 20 = 67$ times

Engage: Answers will vary.

The Mountain that Lost Its Top (pages 13–15)

Problem Solving: 1. Seattle is farther away; 185 miles > 70 miles; $185 - 70 = 115$ miles 2. about 60 days; about 30 days 3. $57 - 27 = 30$ people found dead 4. Drawing should show a small circle around a mountain labeled 8 miles, then another circle labeled 20 miles, and a larger circle around outside of the mountain labeled 230 square miles; 20 miles − 8 miles = 12 miles

Engage: 1. to stay safe; They thought the volcano would erupt. 2. Ash traveled very fast (650 miles per hour) 3. Rocks and ice slid down the mountain at a great speed; it landed in the river, the rivers carried it into the area around the mountain.
4. The east wind blew that day and carried ash far away. 5. 1,300 feet

Spaceship Wars (pages 16–18)

Problem Solving: 1. $2 + 2 + 2 = 6$; 2 2. even; There are two people playing; the cards can be counted in pairs 3. The two spaceship cards had the same power and Anthony and Makayla had a battle; Makayla; $1 + 5 + 1 = 7$; $7 + 7 = 14$ 4. $36 - 27 = 9$; 9; 27 > 9 or 9 < 27

Engage: 1. even 2. odd 3. even 4.–5. Answers will vary.

Twelve Men of Gotham (pages 19–21)

Problem Solving: 1. 12 2. even 3. 11 men; Answers will vary. 4. They counted only 11 people; each man did not count himself. 5. He counted one by one to show them that each one needed to be counted.

Engage: 1. 12 groups of 5 = 60 dollars
2. $12 - 3 = 9$ men; 9 groups of 5 = 45 dollars
3. 6; 18 fish 4. 12 groups of 2 = 24 men; $24 + 1 = 25$ men; odd

A Balloon Ride (pages 22–24)

Problem Solving: 1. 14 people 2. 14 people
3. 19 people 4. 3 feet; 36 inches; Answers will vary. 5. 1 hour; 2–10 miles 6. 500 flights

Engage: 1. basket; burner; envelope 2. the envelope, because it holds air 3. hot air; by going up and down to find air moving in the direction he/she wants to go 4. wind speed 5. Answers will vary.

Waving the Flag (pages 25–27)

Problem Solving: 1. 13 stripes stand for the original colonies; odd 2. $13 + \underline{37} = 50$ or $50 - 13 = \underline{37}$
3. even 4. 9; 4; 5; $5 + 5 + 5 + 5 = 20$; $6 + 6 + 6 + 6 + 6 = 30$; $20 + 30 = 50$ 5. the first flag; when there were 13 colonies 6. 27

Engage: 1. Answers will vary. 2. The USA has added more states. 3.–4. Answers will vary.

Benjamin Banneker: Math Whiz (pages 28–30)

Problem Solving: 1. 100 acres; 50 city blocks; Answers will vary. 2. $21 + \_\_\_ = 59$; 38 years; $59 + \_\_\_ = 74$ years; 15 years; *Suggested answers:* addition and subtraction strategies; grouping by tens 3. 3 rows with 20 marks in each row; $20 each month 4. $1792 + 5$ years $= 1797$ 5. 66 years old $+ \_\_\_ = 74$ years old; 8 years

Engage: 1. a book with tide tables; charts of the sun, moon, and stars, and other information to help farmers 2. He helped survey land for the nation's new capital. 3. Answers will vary. 4. Many copies were printed for people to buy and read.
5. Answers will vary.

Answer Key (cont.)

Riding the School Bus (pages 31–33)

Problem Solving: 1. 5 rows; 4 or 6 depending on number of total seats; an array **2.** 8 rows; 6 kids **3.** 72; 12 rows; 6 kids; 3 seats on each side of the aisle **4.** 38 − 26 = 12 feet; 38 − 28 = 10 feet **5.** 26 feet; 28 feet; 35–38 feet

Engage: 1. to get to school, to go on a field trip, to go to a sports event **2.** rows of seats, an aisle to walk down, windows, a place for the driver **3.** space for wheelchairs, a lift to get wheelchairs into the bus, not as many seats, seat belts **4.–5.** Answers will vary.

The Pied Piper (pages 34–36)

Problem Solving: 1. Answers will vary. **2.** twenty-second; seventy-six; July 22, 1376 **3.** current year − 1376 = Answers will vary. **4.** current year − 1888 = Answers will vary.

Engage: 1. east, west, north, south; He searched in all directions or everywhere. **2.** summer; July **3.** silver and gold **4.** Drawing should show 10 bundles of 100 with 5 circled; 500. **5.** 1,000; 50; 1,000 − 50 = 950

Robin Hood and the Sad Knight (pages 37–39)

Problem Solving: 1. Fourscore; 80 **2.** 10 shillings; 120 pennies **3.** 600 pounds **4.** 400 pounds **5.** 1,000 pounds

Engage: 1. nothing; Robin Hood gave the Knight his money bag back and told him he would help him instead. **2.** across the ocean to fight other battles **3.** His wife will have to live with her family in charity **4.** −**5.** Answers will vary.

The First Post Office (pages 40–42)

Problem Solving: 1. 49 cents; 6 cents; 49 cents − 6 cents = 43 cents; 43 cents + 6 cents = 49 cents **2.** 25 cents; 6 cents; 25 cents − 6 cents = 19 cents; 6 cents + 19 cents = 25 cents **3.** 450 miles; 30 miles; 450 miles − 30 miles = 420 miles **4.** current year − 1792 = Answers will vary.

Engage: *Suggested answers:* **1.** People traveled by foot or horse and it took longer to go a greater distance. **2.** It is easier to charge one price; most mail goes by truck, train, or plane, and they all have fuel costs. **3.** We understand how transportation affects the way we do things; we understand that prices increase. **4.** Other things cost more, too, like gas for a mail truck. The post office is bigger now, and they have to pay more people to work there. **5.** It means that it costs more money now than it did.

Sleeping Lemurs (pages 43–45)

Problem Solving: 1. 41 degrees; 60 degrees; 60 − 41 = 19 degrees **2.** 90 − 41 = 49 degrees **3.** 120 − 6 = 114 beats per minute **4.** (200 + 10 + 7) − (100 + 40 + 2) = 70 + 5; 75 grams

Engage: 1. Its breathing and heart rate slow down; it does not need to eat food; it sleeps and does not move around. **2.** It uses the fat stored in its tail when it hibernates. **3.** The weather is colder, and there is not as much food. **4.** It does not sleep the deep sleep animals need to stay alive; it is not as cold where it lives as it is in places where other animals (like bears) hibernate. **5.** They think people might be able to hibernate in the future.

Lou Gehrig: The Iron Horse of Baseball (pages 46–48)

Problem Solving: 1. Babe Ruth wore number 3, an odd number. Lou Gehrig wore number 4, an even number. **2.** (400 + 90 + 3) − (40 + 9) = 400 + 40 + 4; 444 home runs **3.** 149 − 47 = 102 runs **4.** 185 − 162 = 23 more runs; 162 + 23 = 185

Engage: 1. Lou Gehrig was not as famous as Babe Ruth **2.** first base **3.** He hit many home runs and also helped other players score runs. **4.** He had a mysterious illness. **5.** *Suggested answers:* He was dependable, he worked hard, he didn't quit, he did his best.

Wild Winter Weather (pages 49–51)

Problem Solving: 1. 34 inches; 22 inches; 34 − 22 =12 inches **2.** 16 inches; 5 inches **3.** over 108 inches **4.** 98 inches; Answers will vary. **5.** 108 − 98 = 10 inches

Engage: 1. Boston **2.** A lot of snow fell. **3.** −**6.** Answers will vary.

Small Town U.S.A.: Port Aransas (pages 52–54)

Problem Solving: 1. 8 miles; 18 miles; 8 + ___ = 18 miles; 10 miles **2.** 600 **3.** 450 < 600 or 600 > 450; Port Aransas **4.** 450 fish + ___ = 600 fish; 150 more kinds of fish in Port Aransas **5.** 400 pounds; 100 pounds; 400 − 100 = 300 pounds

Engage: 1. 8 − 2 = 6 boats **2.** 28 + 28 = 56 cars **3.** 20 cars; 28 + 20 + 20 = 68 cars **4.** even **5.** Drawing should show 6 smaller boats with 20 cars each and 2 larger boats with 28 cars each. **6.** Each boat has an equal number of cars in rows.

Answer Key (cont.)

Forest Giants (pages 55–57)

Problem Solving: 1. 1,900 years **2.** 90 – 60 = 30 feet difference in height of maple trees; 100 – 90 = 10 feet difference between a pine tree and a tall maple tree; 100 – 60 = 40 feet difference between a maple tree (not tall) and a pine tree **3.** 364 feet; 310 feet; 300 + 60 + 4; 300 + 10; 364 > 310; The redwood is taller. **4.** 10 feet; 40 feet – 30 = ___ or 30 feet + ___ = 40 feet **5.** 2,000; 3,000; 1,000 years difference; Answers will vary.

Engage: 1. feet; Twelve inches is the same as one foot. **2.** inches **3.** (shortest to tallest) maple, pine, sequoia, redwood; maple; maple and pine

Cyrus McCormick: Help for Farmers (pages 58–60)

Problem Solving: 1. 16 years; 6 weeks; father; 16 years > 6 weeks **2.** 500 reapers; 1,000 reapers; 500 + ___ = 1,000; 500 more machines **3.** 1831 – 22 = 1809 **4.** 1884 – 1809 = 75 years; Answers will vary.

Engage: 1. 1831 – 16 years = 1815 **2.** 1831 + ___ = 1834; 3 years **3.** 1848 – 1809 = 39 years old **4.** 1848 + 3 years = 1851 **5.** They could use the machine and pay later when they sold their crops.

Flying in the Wind (pages 61–63)

Problem Solving: 1. 100 – 50 = 50 feet **2.** 75 – 50 = 25 feet **3.** 600 inches **4.** 50 + 50 + 50 + 50 = 200 feet **5.** 75 + 75 = 150 feet, 100 + 100 = 200 feet **6.** 24 feet

Engage: 1. Students might draw a diamond kite or triangle stunt kite. **2.** Drawings will vary. **3.** centimeters; Answers will vary. **4.** Answers will vary.

Rapunzel (pages 64–66)

Problem Solving: 1. Tower should be labeled as at least 30 feet tall. **2.** 30 feet **3.** 3 feet in a yard; 10 yards **4.** a meter; 10 meters **5.** 100 centimeters; 1,000 centimeters **6.** 3 stories

Engage: 1. Answers will vary but should be close to 30 feet. **2.** No, 47 inches – 6 inches = 41 inches; 41 inches – 36 inches = 5 inches **3.** Answers will vary. **4.** 36 – 24 = 12 inches

Track Meet (pages 67–69)

Problem Solving: 1. 1 minute and 30 seconds; 16 seconds faster; 74 seconds; 4 seconds **2.** 122 inches; 116 inches **3.** Tyler; 6 inches; 122 – 116 = 6 inches

Engage: Answers will vary.

Kart Racing (pages 70–72)

Problem Solving: 1. 15 minutes; 20 minutes; 5 minutes; 20 – 15 = 5 **2.** 45 minutes; 25 minutes; 45 – 20 = 25 **3.** Clocks should show 1:15. **4.** Clocks should show 2:45. **5.** up to 10 minutes; 15 or 20 minutes; 5 or 10 minutes; 10 min. weekend < 15 or 20 min. weekday

Engage: 1. sprint and enduro races; a short race; a longer race on a full-size track **2.** less than 1 mile; 1 or 2 miles or more **3.** the day of the week; how many karts are at the track **4.** 100 miles per hour; faster; Answers will vary. **5.** Answers will vary.

Going to a Market (pages 73–75)

Problem Solving: 1. carrots **2.** carrots, green beans, green peppers, tomatoes; They are all vegetables. **3.** cost less to grow, good weather for those crops, fewer people want to buy and eat those foods **4.** $1.07 + ___ = $1.57; $0.50 or 50¢; $0.57 + ___ = $1.04; $0.47 or 47¢; $0.57 **5.** apples; 3¢ more per pound than oranges **6.** Answers will vary.

Engage: 1. fruits, vegetables, honey, jam, baked goods **2.** It depends on the town—in some places it is one or two days a week. **3.** They plant what will grow in that area; they grow things people want to buy. **4.** People might buy a different kind of fruit instead; people might not buy as much of the item that costs more. **5.** weather, how many people want to buy that fruit or vegetable, how much it costs the farmer to grow the food **6.** They think the food is healthier; they might want to try something different; they want to help local farmers.

A Different Kind of Pet (pages 76–78)

Problem Solving: 1. inches **2.** less than 2 inches **3.** the oscar **4.** angelfish, sun catfish, oscar **5.** goldfish **6.** 2 inches: tetra; 2.5 inches: guppy, zebra danio; 3 inches: penguinfish, black molly, goldfish; 7 inches: clown loach; 8 inches: angelfish; 10 inches: sun catfish; 14 inches: oscar

Engage: 1. < 5 inches: tetra, guppy, zebra danio, penguinfish, black molly, goldfish; 5 – 10 inches: angelfish, sun catfish, clown loach; > 10 inches: oscar **2.** 9 **3.** 4 **4.** 6 – 4 = 2 **5.** 10

Answer Key (cont.)

Lighthouses (pages 79–81)

Problem Solving: 1. octagon and hexagon; octagon has 8; hexagon has 6 **2.** a cylinder **3.** a cone

Engage: Answers will vary.

Sandcastle Fun (pages 82–84)

Problem Solving: 1. cone (funnel); cylinder (round container); cube (sandwich box); Each shape has height and width and depth (three-dimensional). **2.** cube; cone **3.** at the corners of the castle **4.** to show where the drawbridge would rest **5.** hexagon

Engage: Answers will vary.

Energy from the Sun (pages 85–87)

Problem Solving: 1. rectangle **2.** solar cells **3.** a rectangle divided into squares or rectangles **4.** 45 **5.** Answers will vary.

Engage: 1. the sun **2.** the side facing the sun or the roof **3.–5.** Answers will vary.

City Blocks (pages 88–90)

Problem Solving: 1. Each side of the square should be labeled 6 miles. **2.** 36 **3.** 6 sections in a row; 6 rows in a township **4.** 4; one quarter or one fourth **5.** 16

Engage: Answers will vary.

The World of Soccer (pages 91–93)

Problem Solving: 1. one half; each team's half of the playing field, may include goal box and penalty box **2.** one fourth or one quarter; Answers will vary—may include goal box and penalty box. **3.** one half; one team's part of the center circle **4.** one fourth or one quarter; corner arcs

Engage: 1. kickoff to start the game **2.** goalie **3.** The goal box is inside the penalty box. **4.** Goalies can touch the ball with their hands; players make fouls against opponents. **5.** Players take a corner kick to put the ball back into play after it goes out of bounds at the end line.

Tasty Cornbread (pages 94–96)

Problem Solving: 1. a round or rectangle shape **2.** round **3.** Answers will vary. **4.** 4 pieces **5.** 2 pieces or one half of the cornbread **6.** one quarter or one fourth of the cornbread

Engage: 1. The small cake could be baked on the flat metal part of a garden hoe. **2.** It is made with things people have on hand. **3.** seeds, nuts, berries, milk, butter, eggs, sugar, honey, molasses **4.** Answers will vary.

Movie Day (pages 97–99)

Problem Solving: 1. 3; in thirds; one third; Drawing should show a blanket with 3 children on it. **2.** 3; one third; Drawing should show 3 bowls of popcorn. **3.** so each child would have an equal amount of space **4.** 4; one fourth or one quarter; Drawing should show a circle divided into fourths.

Engage: 1. Picture should show a square, rectangle, or circle divided into thirds. **2.** one third **3.** two thirds **4.** 4 **5.** one fourth or one quarter

George Washington Carver: Not Just Peanut Butter (pages 100–102)

Problem Solving: 1. oval **2.** cylinder; round sides; circular ends (faces) that are the same size **3.** things that come in a jar or can: jam, pickles, salsa, etc. **4.** Answers will vary.

Engage: 1. He taught them to use their land better. **2.** to not grow the same thing in the same field each year **3.** cotton; An insect ate the cotton, and they needed to make money. **4.** sweet potatoes, peanuts, and soy beans **5.** cooking oil, dyes for clothes, plastic, peanut butter

Meeting Standards

Each unit meets one or more of the following Common Core State Standards (© Copyright 2010. National Governors Association Center for Best Practices and Council of Chief State School Officers. All rights reserved.) For more information about the Common Core State Standards, go to *http://www.corestandards.org/* or *http://www.teachercreated.com/standards/*.

MATH	
Operations & Algebraic Thinking	
Represent and solve problems involving addition and subtraction.	**Unit**
CCSS.Math.Content.2.OA.A.1: Use addition and subtraction within 100 to solve one- and two-step word problems involving situations of adding to, taking from, putting together, taking apart, and comparing, with unknowns in all positions.	The Blue Angels A Day at the Playground The Mountain that Lost Its Top Spaceship Wars Twelve Men of Gotham A Balloon Ride Waving the Flag Benjamin Banneker: Math Whiz Riding the School Bus The First Post Office Sleeping Lemurs Lou Gehrig: The Iron Horse of Baseball Wild Winter Weather Small Town U.S.A.: Port Aransas Forest Giants Rapunzel Kart Racing Going to a Market Lighthouses
Add and subtract within 20.	**Unit**
CCSS.Math.Content.2.OA.B.2: Fluently add and subtract within 20 using mental strategies. By end of Grade 2, know from memory all sums of two one-digit numbers.	The Blue Angels A Day at the Playground The Mountain that Lost Its Top Spaceship Wars Twelve Men of Gotham A Balloon Ride Wild Winter Weather Small Town U.S.A.: Port Aransas
Work with equal groups of objects to gain foundations for multiplication.	**Unit**
CCSS.Math.Content.2.OA.C.3: Determine whether a group of objects (up to 20) has an odd or even number of members, e.g., by pairing objects or counting them by 2s; write an equation to express an even number as a sum of two equal addends.	The Blue Angels A Day at the Playground Spaceship Wars Twelve Men of Gotham A Balloon Ride Waving the Flag Benjamin Banneker: Math Whiz Small Town U.S.A.: Port Aransas
CCSS.Math.Content.2.OA.C.4: Use addition to find the total number of objects arranged in rectangular arrays with up to 5 rows and up to 5 columns; write an equation to express the total as a sum of equal addends.	Twelve Men of Gotham Waving the Flag Benjamin Banneker: Math Whiz Riding the School Bus Robin Hood and the Sad Knight Small Town U.S.A.: Port Aransas Flying in the Wind Energy from the Sun City Blocks
Number & Operations in Base Ten	
Understand place value.	**Unit**
CCSS.Math.Content.2.NBT.A.1: Understand that the three digits of a three-digit number represent amounts of hundreds, tens, and ones; e.g., 706 equals 7 hundreds, 0 tens, and 6 ones. Understand the following as special cases: **A:** 100 can be thought of as a bundle of ten tens—called a "hundred." **B:** The numbers 100, 200, 300, 400, 500, 600, 700, 800, 900 refer to one, two, three, four, five, six, seven, eight, or nine hundreds (and 0 tens and 0 ones).	The Mountain that Lost Its Top Robin Hood and the Sad Knight Sleeping Lemurs Lou Gehrig: The Iron Horse of Baseball Small Town U.S.A.: Port Aransas Forest Giants

Meeting Standards (cont.)

Number & Operations in Base Ten (cont.)

Understand place value. (cont)	Unit
CCSS.Math.Content.2.NBT.A.2: Count within 1000; skip-count by 5s, 10s, and 100s.	Twelve Men of Gotham Robin Hood and the Sad Knight Forest Giants
CCSS.Math.Content.2.NBT.A.3: Read and write numbers to 1000 using base-ten numerals, number names, and expanded form.	The Pied Piper Forest Giants Cyrus McCormick: Help for Farmers Energy from the Sun
CCSS.Math.Content.2.NBT.A.4: Compare two three-digit numbers based on meanings of the hundreds, tens, and ones digits, using >, =, and < symbols to record the results of comparisons.	The Mountain that Lost Its Top Small Town U.S.A.: Port Aransas Forest Giants Going to a Market

Use place value understanding and properties of operations to add and subtract.	Unit
CCSS.Math.Content.2.NBT.B.5: Fluently add and subtract within 100 using strategies based on place value, properties of operations, and/or the relationship between addition and subtraction.	The Blue Angels The Mountain that Lost Its Top Benjamin Banneker: Math Whiz Robin Hood and the Sad Knight The First Post Office Sleeping Lemurs Lou Gehrig: The Iron Horse of Baseball Wild Winter Weather Small Town U.S.A.: Port Aransas Forest Giants Rapunzel Going to a Market Lighthouses
CCSS.Math.Content.2.NBT.B.6: Add up to four two-digit numbers using strategies based on place value and properties of operations.	Wild Winter Weather
CCSS.Math.Content.2.NBT.B.7: Add and subtract within 1000, using concrete models or drawings and strategies based on place value, properties of operations, and/or the relationship between addition and subtraction; relate the strategy to a written method. Understand that in adding or subtracting three-digit numbers, one adds or subtracts hundreds and hundreds, tens and tens, ones and ones; and sometimes it is necessary to compose or decompose tens or hundreds.	Benjamin Banneker: Math Whiz The Pied Piper Robin Hood and the Sad Knight The First Post Office Sleeping Lemurs Lou Gehrig: The Iron Horse of Baseball Forest Giants Cyrus McCormick: Help for Farmers
CCSS.Math.Content.2.NBT.B.8: Mentally add 10 or 100 to a given number 100–900, and mentally subtract 10 or 100 from a given number 100–900.	Forest Giants Flying in the Wind Kart Racing Energy from the Sun
CCSS.Math.Content.2.NBT.B.9: Explain why addition and subtraction strategies work, using place value and the properties of operations.	Benjamin Banneker: Math Whiz Wild Winter Weather Forest Giants Cyrus McCormick: Help for Farmers

Measurement & Data

Measure and estimate lengths in standard units.	Unit
CCSS.Math.Content.2.MD.A.1: Measure the length of an object by selecting and using appropriate tools such as rulers, yardsticks, meter sticks, and measuring tapes.	The Blue Angels Rapunzel A Different Kind of Pet Tasty Cornbread
CCSS.Math.Content.2.MD.A.3: Estimate lengths using units of inches, feet, centimeters, and meters.	The Blue Angels Forest Giants Flying in the Wind Rapunzel
CCSS.Math.Content.2.MD.A.4: Measure to determine how much longer one object is than another, expressing the length difference in terms of a standard length unit.	Riding the School Bus Flying in the Wind A Different Kind of Pet

Measurement & Data *(cont.)*	
Relate addition and subtraction to length.	**Unit**
CCSS.Math.Content.2.MD.B.5: Use addition and subtraction within 100 to solve word problems involving lengths that are given in the same units, e.g., by using drawings (such as drawings of rulers) and equations with a symbol for the unknown number to represent the problem.	Riding the School Bus Forest Giants Flying in the Wind Rapunzel
CCSS.Math.Content.2.MD.B.6: Represent whole numbers as lengths from 0 on a number line diagram with equally spaced points corresponding to the numbers 0, 1, 2, ..., and represent whole-number sums and differences within 100 on a number line diagram.	Flying in the Wind A Different Kind of Pet
Work with time and money.	**Unit**
CCSS.Math.Content.2.MD.C.7: Tell and write time from analog and digital clocks to the nearest five minutes using a.m. and p.m.	Kart Racing
CCSS.Math.Content.2.MD.C.8: Solve word problems involving dollar bills, quarters, dimes, nickels, and pennies, using $ and ¢ symbols appropriately. Example: If you have 2 dimes and 3 pennies, how many cents do you have?	Going to a Market
Represent and interpret data	**Unit**
CCSS.Math.Content.2.MD.D.9: Generate measurement data by measuring lengths of several objects to the nearest whole unit, or by making repeated measurements of the same object. Show the measurements by making a line plot, where the horizontal scale is marked off in whole-number units.	A Different Kind of Pet
CCSS.Math.Content.2.MD.D.10: Draw a picture graph and a bar graph (with single-unit scale) to represent a data set with up to four categories. Solve simple put-together, take-apart, and compare problems using information presented in a bar graph.	A Different Kind of Pet

Geometry	
Reason with shapes and their attributes.	**Unit**
CCSS.Math.Content.2.G.A.1: Recognize and draw shapes having specified attributes, such as a given number of angles or a given number of equal faces. Identify triangles, quadrilaterals pentagons, hexagons, and cubes.	Lighthouses Sandcastle Fun The World of Soccer George Washington Carver: Not Just Peanut Butter
CCSS.Math.Content.2.G.A.2: Partition a rectangle into rows and columns of same-size squares and count to find the total number of them.	Energy from the Sun City Blocks
CCSS.Math.Content.2.G.A.3: Partition circles and rectangles into two, three, or four equal shares, describe the shares using the words halves, thirds, half of, a third of, etc., and describe the whole as two halves, three thirds, four fourths. Recognize that equal shares of identical wholes need not have the same shape.	The World of Soccer Tasty Cornbread Movie Day George Washington Carver: Not Just Peanut Butter

ENGLISH LANGUAGE ARTS	
Reading: Literature	
Key Ideas and Details	**Unit**
CCSS.ELA-Literacy.RL.2.1: Ask and answer such questions as *who, what, where, when, why,* and *how* to demonstrate understanding of key details in a text.	A Day at the Playground Spaceship Wars Twelve Men of Gotham Waving the Flag Benjamin Banneker: Math Whiz The Pied Piper Robin Hood and the Sad Knight Lou Gehrig: The Iron Horse of Baseball Cyrus McCormick: Help for Farmers Rapunzel Sandcastle Fun Movie Day George Washington Carver: Not Just Peanut Butter
CCSS.ELA-Literacy.RL.2.2: Recount stories, including fables and folktales from diverse cultures, and determine their central message, lesson, or moral.	Twelve Men of Gotham Waving the Flag Robin Hood and the Sad Knight

Meeting Standards *(cont.)*

<table>
<tr><td colspan="2" align="center">Reading: Literature (cont.)</td></tr>
<tr><td align="center">Key Ideas and Details (cont.)</td><td align="center">Unit</td></tr>
<tr>
<td>CCSS.ELA-Literacy.RL.2.3: Describe how characters in a story respond to major events and challenges.</td>
<td>Spaceship Wars
The Pied Piper
Robin Hood and the Sad Knight
Lou Gehrig:
    The Iron Horse of Baseball
Sandcastle Fun
Movie Day
George Washington Carver:
    Not Just Peanut Butter</td>
</tr>
<tr><td align="center">Integration of Knowledge and Ideas</td><td align="center">Unit</td></tr>
<tr>
<td>CCSS.ELA-Literacy.RL.2.7: Use information gained from the illustrations and words in a print or digital text to demonstrate understanding of its characters, setting, or plot.</td>
<td>A Day at the Playground
Waving the Flag
Lou Gehrig:
    The Iron Horse of Baseball
Sandcastle Fun
Energy from the Sun</td>
</tr>
<tr><td colspan="2" align="center">Reading: Informational Text</td></tr>
<tr><td align="center">Key Ideas and Details</td><td align="center">Unit</td></tr>
<tr>
<td>CCSS.ELA-Literacy.RI.2.1: Ask and answer such questions as who, what, where, when, why, and how to demonstrate understanding of key details in a text.</td>
<td>The Blue Angels
The Mountain that Lost Its Top
A Balloon Ride
Riding the School Bus
The First Post Office
Sleeping Lemurs
Wild Winter Weather
Small Town U.S.A.: Port Aransas
Forest Giants
Flying in the Wind
Kart Racing
Going to a Market
A Different Kind of Pet
Lighthouses
Energy from the Sun
City Blocks
The World of Soccer
Tasty Cornbread</td>
</tr>
<tr>
<td>CCSS.ELA-Literacy.RI.2.3: Describe the connection between a series of historical events, scientific ideas or concepts, or steps in technical procedures in a text.</td>
<td>The Mountain that Lost Its Top
A Balloon Ride
Benjamin Banneker: Math Whiz
Riding the School Bus
The First Post Office
Sleeping Lemurs
Lou Gehrig:
    The Iron Horse of Baseball
Small Town U.S.A.: Port Aransas
Cyrus McCormick: Help for Farmers
Kart Racing
Going to a Market
Energy from the Sun
City Blocks
The World of Soccer
Tasty Cornbread
George Washington Carver:
    Not Just Peanut Butter</td>
</tr>
</table>

Meeting Standards *(cont.)*

Craft and Structure	Unit

CCSS.ELA-Literacy.RI.2.4: Determine the meaning of words and phrases in a text relevant to a *grade 2 topic or subject area.*	The Blue Angels
	The Mountain that Lost Its Top
	A Balloon Ride
	Benjamin Banneker: Math Whiz
	Riding the School Bus
	Robin Hood and the Sad Knight
	Sleeping Lemurs
	Lou Gehrig:
	    The Iron Horse of Baseball
	Small Town U.S.A.: Port Aransas
	Forest Giants
	Cyrus McCormick: Help for Farmers
	Kart Racing
	Going to a Market
	A Different Kind of Pet
	Lighthouses
	Energy from the Sun
	City Blocks
	The World of Soccer
	George Washington Carver:
	    Not Just Peanut Butter

CCSS.ELA-Literacy.RI.2.5: Know and use various text features (e.g., captions, bold print, subheadings, glossaries, indexes, electronic menus, icons) to locate key facts or information in a text efficiently.	Going to a Market

Integration of Knowledge and Ideas	Unit
CCSS.ELA-Literacy.RI.2.7: Explain how specific images (e.g., a diagram showing how a machine works) contribute to and clarify a text.	The Blue Angels Flying in the Wind A Different Kind of Pet Lighthouses Energy from the Sun City Blocks The World of Soccer
CCSS.ELA-Literacy.RI.2.8: Describe how reasons support specific points the author makes in a text.	Riding the School Bus Sleeping Lemurs Small Town U.S.A.: Port Aransas Going to a Market Tasty Cornbread George Washington Carver: Not Just Peanut Butter

Writing

Text Types and Purposes	Unit
CCSS.ELA-Literacy.W.2.1: Write opinion pieces in which they introduce the topic or book they are writing about, state an opinion, supply reasons that support the opinion, use linking words (e.g., *because, and, also*) to connect opinion and reasons, and provide a concluding statement or section.	The Blue Angels A Balloon Ride Waving the Flag Benjamin Banneker: Math Whiz Riding the School Bus The Pied Piper Robin Hood and the Sad Knight The First Post Office Lou Gehrig: The Iron Horse of Baseball Kart Racing City Blocks Tasty Cornbread

Writing *(cont.)*	
Text Types and Purposes *(cont.)*	Unit
CCSS.ELA-Literacy.W.2.2: Write informative/explanatory texts in which they introduce a topic, use facts and definitions to develop points, and provide a concluding statement or section.	The Mountain that Lost Its Top Spaceship Wars Twelve Men of Gotham The First Post Office Sleeping Lemurs Wild Winter Weather Small Town U.S.A.: Port Aransas Forest Giants Kart Racing A Different Kind of Pet The World of Soccer Tasty Cornbread George Washington Carver: Not Just Peanut Butter
CCSS.ELA-Literacy.W.2.3: Write narratives in which they recount a well-elaborated event or short sequence of events, include details to describe actions, thoughts, and feelings, use temporal words to signal event order, and provide a sense of closure.	Wild Winter Weather Tasty Cornbread
Research to Build and Present Knowledge	Unit
CCSS.ELA-Literacy.W.2.7: Participate in shared research and writing projects (e.g., read a number of books on a single topic to produce a report; record science observations).	The Blue Angels Waving the Flag Wild Winter Weather Kart Racing Lighthouses The World of Soccer George Washington Carver: Not Just Peanut Butter

CCSS.ELA-Literacy.W.2.8: Recall information from experiences or gather information from provided sources to answer a question.	The Blue Angels
	A Day at the Playground
	The Mountain that Lost Its Top
	Spaceship Wars
	A Balloon Ride
	Waving the Flag
	Benjamin Banneker: Math Whiz
	Riding the School Bus
	Robin Hood and the Sad Knight
	Sleeping Lemurs
	Lou Gehrig:
	   The Iron Horse of Baseball
	Wild Winter Weather
	Flying in the Wind
	Rapunzel
	Kart Racing
	Going to a Market
	A Different Kind of Pet
	Lighthouses
	Sandcastle Fun
	Energy from the Sun
	City Blocks
	The World of Soccer
	Tasty Cornbread
	Movie Day
	George Washington Carver:
	   Not Just Peanut Butter